JOHN CLARKE has completed studies and research in Psychology in the areas of psychopaths in the workplace, criminal profiling, serial rape, animal cruelty offenders and sexual homicide crime scene analysis. He works as a consultant to corporations experiencing problems with a suspected workplace psychopath, as well as with victims of workplace psychopaths. He has also worked as a consultant for the NSW Police in developing offender profiles. He has lectured on psychopaths in the work-place, criminal profiling, abnormal psychology and criminal psychology at the University of Sydney, as well as to members of various law enforcement agencies, legal practitioners and psychologists. John has commented on criminal psychology and workplace psychopaths in print media, radio and television, both in Australia and over-seas. Further information on workplace psychopaths and related topics can be found at www.drjohnclarke.com.

Working *with* Monsters

How to identify and protect yourself
from the workplace psychopath

John Clarke

RANDOM HOUSE AUSTRALIA

The advice and strategies discussed in this book are intended as a guideline only. In some cases it is advisable to seek professional advice.

While all the cases referred to in this book are real, the names, locations and occupations of some of the people described have been changed to protect their identities. No dramatisation or exaggeration of cases has been added. Any resemblance to real persons, either living or dead, as a result of these changes is purely coincidental.

Random House Australia Pty Ltd
100 Pacific Highway, North Sydney, NSW 2060
http://www.randomhouse.com.au

Sydney   New York   Toronto
London   Auckland   Johannesburg

First published by Random House Australia 2005

National Library of Australia
Cataloguing-in-Publication Entry

Clarke, John, 1976– .
Working with monsters.

Bibliography.
ISBN 978 1 74051 154 4.
ISBN 1 74051 154 9.

1. Psychopaths – Australia. 2. Antisocial personality
disorders. 3. Bullying in the workplace – Australia –
Prevention. 4. Intimidation – Australia – Prevention.
I. Title.

658.31450994

Cover image by Getty Images
Cover and internal design by Darian Causby/Highway 51 Design Works
Typeset by Midland Typesetters, Maryborough, Victoria
Printed and bound by Griffin Press, South Australia

CONTENTS

8 • Workplace Psychopaths — Are They Good for Business? • 165

9 • The Human Cost of Workplace Psychopaths • 181

10 • Protecting Yourself • 199

11 • Profiling the Psychopath and the Organisation • 231

12 • Mistaken Identity — Alternative Diagnoses • 260

'Hell is not in torture;
Hell is in an empty heart.'

Kahlil Gibran, *The Prophet*

PROLOGUE

THE LAST TIME I saw Charlotte was on a cold, miserable day in her office. She was doomed to a form of hell, devoid of feelings for other people, unable to experience true love or friendship, honesty or compassion, joy or sorrow. Charlotte had no conscience; she could not empathise with or understand others. She had been referred to me one year earlier by her company director, and in that time she took me on a journey to a place difficult even to imagine, a place in which she devoured the very essence of people's psyches, destroying their spirit for her own psychological gratification. Charlotte was a predator ruthlessly using her charm, beauty, intelligence and exceptional manipulative skills to completely dominate and destroy the people she worked with. Charlotte, without question, was a workplace psychopath.

Psychopaths are people who lack a conscience,

they live in their own complex world where society's rules are broken at will. Dr Robert Hare, Professor Emeritus of Psychology at the University of British Columbia, has researched psychopaths for more than twenty-five years and has described them as 'social predators who charm, manipulate and ruthlessly plow their way through life, leaving a broad trail of broken hearts, shattered expectations and empty wallets... selfishly taking what they want and doing as they please without the slightest sense of guilt or regret' (Hare, 1993, p. xi).

The term psychopath usually conjures images of serial killers and rapists, members of a criminal world few people ever come into contact with. But contrary to popular stereotypes, the majority of psychopaths are not homicidal maniacs or sexual deviants. People who display all the hallmarks of a psychopath work and operate unchallenged in society and are found in areas as diverse as medicine, law enforcement, the stock exchange, schools, universities, sales, advertising and construction, to name but a few. They make up approximately 1 to 3 per cent of the adult male population and 0.5 to 1 per cent of the adult female population and can work as mechanics or lawyers, in factories or corporate boardrooms, for the government or in private industry. Everyone, at some stage in their life is highly likely to encounter a psychopath, whether it be a 'colleague' at work, a person living in your street, or the con artist who knocks on your door.

Through my work as a consultant psychological profiler for both the NSW Police in criminal matters and with corporations who are experiencing difficulties with an employee, I have dealt with many clients similar to Charlotte. Male and female. Young and old. People from all walks of life. They are not all the same: some have committed murder, or raped one or perhaps many people; others have psychologically destroyed people they work with or those unfortunate enough to be their employees; many have defrauded their employers or members of society not only of millions of dollars, but also of their trust; and some have held positions of authority and harmed the very people they were supposed to protect. Each of these groups is characterised by different manifestations of the same disorder – psychopathy.

Working with Monsters is a journey through the frightful darkness of the psychopathic mind. It pays particular attention to the workplace psychopath, which has not been covered in depth before. Some people may doubt that these predators exist in workplaces across Australia, and indeed across the globe. I can assure you, from my consulting work with many corporations, large and small, domestic and multinational, they do exist and are a significant problem. If left unchecked, the workplace psychopath has the ability to create immense devastation in their unfortunate victims' lives as well as bring a company down.

Most people don't recognise psychopaths for what they are until it is too late, however a working knowledge of how they operate can provide you with the best possible weapon against the psychopath, wherever you may encounter them. *Working with Monsters* answers a number of questions that are important to identifying, understanding and subsequently dealing with the psychopath, including: What is a psychopath? Is it possible to detect a psychopathic personality? Does the psychopath behave noticeably differently compared to the 'normal' person? How do they conceal themselves so well? Do they process information about the world in a different way to you or I? What strategies do they employ to achieve what they want and what do they desire in life? How is it possible for a person to become so disconnected from other people as to lose all empathy? Are psychopaths born or are they made by our society? What can we do to change them, or are they incurable? By answering these questions I hope to give people the knowledge required to guard against an under-recognised danger within our society.

The scientific, psychological approach adopted in the book comes from my academic background in forensic psychology at the University of Sydney. The more applied sections represent my involvement in criminal psychological profiling for law enforcement agencies, a diverse range of victim support groups, and as a consultant to numerous corporations and individuals who have experienced problems identifying and dealing with a psychopath within their midst. This combination of academic and practical experience has proved invaluable to me in understanding psychopathy, and in sharing both perspectives I hope that they provide some benefit to you personally and society in general.

1

INTRODUCTION TO A MONSTER

THE LOWEST POINT of my journey into the mind of a white-collar psychopath was when I met Wayne. Never before had I encountered such a destructive individual. He was a remorseless human predator who stopped at nothing in his never-ending hunt for power and control. Bullying, intimidation, impulsive outbursts, manipulative and insincere behaviours were typical when it came to achieving what he wanted. When I began my research for my PhD, I examined serial killers, rapists, stalkers and child abusers, and Wayne displayed characteristics remarkably similar to these violent criminals. He regarded himself as the fittest species in a corporate jungle where only the strongest, most brutal survived. In reality he was ruthlessly trying to quench an insatiable appetite for power and control, and he delighted in psychologically weakening and then devouring those he saw as prey; his employees and colleagues. Wayne was without conscience.

Today my area of expertise is in offender psychological profiling, whether that be profiling serious violent criminals or workplace psychopaths. I have discovered that there is very little difference between compiling a psychological profile of a serial rapist and developing a profile of an organisational psychopath. Once the primary motivating factor of power and self-gratification is understood, it is simply a matter of following the path of destruction left by both types of psychopath.

Wayne was a classic example of a particularly malevolent type of psychopath found in the workplace. Operating at a very high level in a successful company, he exuded an almost indefinable, venomous feeling of menace, camouflaged beneath a deceptively smooth but entirely artificial veneer of sophisticated charm. There was a chilling absence of any emotion in his eyes, which seemed to take in and evaluate everything at a glance. What concerned me most was that the expression in his eyes never really changed, it remained devoid of the quality that makes us human – emotion. His unrelenting gaze was a clear message to me about who he believed was in control of our meetings. He grandiosely thought it was him; in his mind it was inconceivable that it could be anyone else. Wayne's trait of self-important egocentrism, of only being concerned with himself, was part of his psychopathic personality. Ultimately it was this that brought Wayne down and he eventually resigned.

Unfortunately, Wayne's departure did nothing for the victims he left in his wake. His legacy to the company was a string of devastating sexual affairs, financial irregularities, shattered emotions, and for many of his ill-fated victims a feeling of utter hopelessness about their ability to function in life. Wayne is one of many psychopaths wreaking untold psychological havoc within companies not only in Australia, but throughout the world.

I met Wayne, a senior partner in a professional firm, as part of my consulting work. He was in charge of close to eighty employees and earned a six-figure base salary, plus his share of the company's profits depending on performance. He gloated in our first meeting that in the previous year he had taken home almost $500,000 because most of the company's business was due to his incredible ability. Wayne had been with the company for the past eight years, and in that short time he had worked his way up to a senior partnership and claimed he had doubled their revenue. At the same time, staff in his section were resigning at unprecedented levels. At one stage in an eighteen-month period, 75 per cent of his staff walked out, many for medical reasons. Wayne justified this unusually high staff turnover rate to the other partners by saying that his was a high-stress work environment because he worked 'his people' extremely hard, and that was how he achieved his excellent results for the company. Considering profits had increased in Wayne's section, the other partners in the company chose to take his word for it.

It was not until the company was forced to settle with an emotionally destroyed ex-employee for a large sum of money that they became concerned and started asking other ex-staff members from Wayne's section why they had resigned. The partners discovered an intricate web of lies and deceit, fabricated by Wayne to ensure that he was always in control. Extraordinary stories of sexual abuse, intimidation, extreme workplace bullying, unethical behaviour and incredible manipulative strategies emerged from the accounts of his shattered victims. His colleagues were stunned by the extent of Wayne's psychopathic behaviour. Wayne had seemed so normal to them; a high achiever who they believed had performed splendidly for the past eight years. It was easy to see how they had been deceived.

At first glance, Wayne was impressive. Attractive and well groomed, Wayne made a point of telling me that he wore only Armani suits that had been custom-made in Italy. He also told me that he drove expensive cars, had a house in a very affluent area of the city and owned a luxury yacht. The image he presented to the world was one of success. In our first meeting he was very well spoken, polite and professed to know about a wide range of topics. His knowledge turned out to be superficial. For example, he tried to impress me by speaking about a range of psychology related topics. When I quizzed him about the very basic psychology he claimed to know so much about, he gave wildly inaccurate responses, before attempting very smoothly to steer our conversation in another direction.

This classic strategy of shifting rapidly from one topic to the next is designed to camouflage the psychopath's lies by causing confusion. By talking only briefly about any one topic, the victim assumes the psychopath is knowledgeable and is not given the opportunity to recognise that all they really know are superficial facts about each topic. For people unaware of this strategy, a person such as Wayne can appear very sophisticated. The staff that had worked with Wayne, as well as the senior partners in the firm, all attested to the effectiveness of this technique. They had been duped into believing that Wayne was extremely knowledgeable about such topics as psychology, philosophy, law, art, politics, history and the environment. In reality, he wasn't knowledgeable, he was just a very good talker.

Wayne's business practices were abysmal, his ethical standards noticeable by their absence. He would lie outright to clients, promising them services he knew his firm could never deliver, and he would do anything to close a deal. His unethical behaviour did not trouble him at all. In fact, it gave him great delight and a sense of pride that he could always manipulate people to get what he wanted. He enjoyed placing his staff under a great deal of unnecessary stress. One of his favourite strategies was to set an unachievable task for someone, bully him or her into completing it, and then tell the employee that it was too late and all the effort they had put in was for nothing. This satisfied his need to humiliate people. Psychologists have found that repeatedly inducing 'learned helplessness', which will be explored more fully later, is an extremely effective way to psychologically 'break' a person, commonly causing them to become depressed or anxious. When Wayne's employees objected to his behaviour, he would add a note to their personnel file describing them as 'uncooperative and difficult to work with' in case they became a threat sometime in the future.

Without exception, Wayne evaluated co-workers in terms of how he could use them and what level of threat they posed to his position and prospects for promotion. He would write notes for himself summarising the strengths and weaknesses of colleagues, and he genuinely could not comprehend why anyone would care about the wellbeing of his employees. For Wayne, the people who worked for him were his property, and it was intolerable to have someone like me interfering with and questioning the techniques he used to control 'his staff'. Throughout our sessions he continued to talk with me about his workplace practices because he hoped to discover who in the company was 'out to get him'. He did not appreciate that he was revealing much more about himself than he realised in each of our meetings.

Wayne was an expert when it came to redirecting blame away from himself when anything went wrong. If he was questioned about why his work was not finished or below standard (as it often was), he would insist that meetings with all the appropriate people be scheduled. He told me that he would never attend these meetings if more than one important person at a time was there, instead he preferred to 'take care of people' individually, on a 'face-to-face' basis. This strategy allowed him to blame other sections or people in the company for his mistakes, knowing that the division or people being blamed would not have the opportunity to defend themselves. This guaranteed that blame was always diverted away from himself. He knew that if he attended a meeting where everyone involved was present, it would be impossible to spread such confusion within the company about why jobs he was responsible for were not being completed. In the end, no one knew exactly who was to blame for a job not being finished, and Wayne would be forgotten, allowing him to move on to engineer the next crisis.

Naturally, Wayne was universally disliked and feared by the junior staff who worked not only in his section, but also by those working in other divisions of the company. He was deceitful, telling people their work was inadequate and then presenting the very same 'inadequate' work as his own to both senior partners and clients. The psychopathy literature refers to this type of behaviour as parasitic, feeding off the work of others to benefit in some way. However, his parasitic behaviour was not limited to work. Wayne would borrow money from his family and friends, never intending to pay them back, despite the fact that he earned a large salary. Wayne also forced his wife to work, so that he could use her money to gamble at the casino, 'satisfy himself' at 'escort agencies', and wine and dine women from work in expensive restaurants. Wayne told me about this aspect of his life as though it were completely acceptable behaviour. His total lack of remorse is a classic characteristic of the psychopath. In fact, rather than feeling guilt, Wayne was quite proud of his ability to spend his wife's money on such activities; it reinforced in his mind how unintelligent she was for allowing it to happen. It also made him feel in complete control of the relationship because he had the power to make her work and then spend her money on activities that she would definitely not have approved of, yet in his mind there was absolutely nothing she could do about it.

Wayne was egotistical and insensitive at work, deliberately humiliating his staff in front of others in the firm. He was unpredictable, one minute acting quite calmly, the next flying into a rage. The ability to rapidly shift from one emotion to another is characteristic of the psychopath. These 'shallow emotions' are turned on or off at the whim of the psychopath because he or she is never really experiencing the bodily sensations associated with emotion. Instead, the psychopath experiences an emotion that is largely cognitive (or mental) in nature. In Wayne's case, the unpredictable and aggressive outbursts were consciously used to keep everyone in a constant state of high anxiety, always on alert for another episode. Every employee desperately hoped they were not going to be the next target of Wayne's fury. Many workplace psychopaths use this unpredictable shifting between emotions as a weapon to make sure they maintain control of the people around them.

Wayne had absolutely no remorse for how he made people feel, lies were a tool to get what he wanted and stay in control, and he would use his intimidating presence with his contrived rages to make certain he was feared by his staff. When I asked him how he thought his staff was responding to his management style, he emphasised that he had other problems to worry about and did not give the staff much thought. When I pressed him on this point, he finally said that if they let themselves be treated as they were, they deserved everything they got because they were weak. Wayne believed that he had the right to do whatever was necessary to come out on top, regardless of the consequences for other people.

I would say it went deeper than this. Not only was Wayne fully aware of the heartache he was responsible for, he thrived on it. His workplace was a hothouse of pain and emotional suffering in which he fed off his employees' misery. For him, the suffering and degradation of his staff produced the same feelings as those experienced by a sexually sadistic rapist who mercilessly tortures his victims. What is important to both is the feeling of power and control that comes from psychologically dominating their victims. The difference is that workplace psychopaths largely dominate their victims using purely psychological rather than physical and psychological techniques.

One particularly important question concerns how Wayne was able to reach such a senior position within a prestigious company. It may surprise you to know that for a psychopath it is not overly difficult to rise to very high levels in certain corporations, particularly in today's uncertain and constantly changing corporate climate. The psychopath revels in job interviews, role-plays and psychometric testing. Once inside the company, they employ a unique set of strategies designed to elevate them to the very top. Wayne set in place a series of manipulative and deceitful strategies from his first day at the company. He played people against each other. He told me that he 'psycho-analysed' the people he worked with, looking for a weak spot. Once he had figured out what they needed psychologically, he gave it to them. After they trusted and depended on him, he was in control, and it was then that he exploited their weak points for his own advantage.

His first act when he arrived at the company was to become 'a leader among men' in the office. He did this by encouraging the other men to isolate and then harass Susan, an overweight female colleague. This common goal unified the men under Wayne's leadership. He also socialised with the men after work, and was described by workmates at that time as 'good for a laugh', 'someone you could depend on', and 'exciting to be with, there was a real buzz in the air whenever Wayne was around'. Researchers in social psychology have found that when a group of people have a common goal, in this case harassing Susan, a strong bond develops between group members. Wayne provided leadership and direction for the group so effectively that his university-educated colleagues did not consider what they were doing to the unfortunate Susan, who had once been a close colleague. Instead they focused on being accepted by Wayne as well as proving themselves in front of their fellow workmates. After all, they had seen the psychological devastation Wayne could bring on a person if he did not like you.

This is a good example of how manipulative the workplace psychopath can be. In effect, Wayne had identified that his colleagues' collective weak point was insecurity about their position and status in life, which he then systematically exploited by making them feel important. Only after they were included in his group did they realise that if they left they would be destroyed by their former colleagues, yet to stay in the group required them to perform behaviours they would usually abhor, such as bullying Susan to the point of her developing depression and leaving the company. Wayne's power over them was such that they chose to go against their beliefs and morals. This ability to pervert people's beliefs about themselves and their world is not uncommon amongst psychopaths, they are masters at manipulating others to suit their own ends. What starts out as voluntary victim behaviour usually ends as fear-driven victim behaviour. In this case, voluntarily harassing Susan turned rapidly into conforming with the group under Wayne's leadership for fear of the consequences.

At this stage, while Wayne was accepted as a friend and leader by the men in the office, he also went to his (and their) boss saying that his co-workers were lazy and incompetent and that he was sick of covering for them. He would show his boss work that his colleagues had done making out that it was his own (early parasitic behaviour). He would express frustration at being so junior in the company when he had such a wealth of ideas and talent that could be used if only the people in charge were not so limited as to stifle his creative abilities (grandiose sense of importance to the company). His boss was taken in and recommended him for fast acceleration through the company (manipulative and deceitful). Incidentally, like so many other workplace psychopaths, Wayne had scored very well on the intelligence and personality tests he was required to take before he entered the company, and his résumé was rated as 'outstanding' by the human resources manager.

At the same time that Wayne was maintaining the façade of friendliness and professionalism toward his boss, he was also writing reports to the human resources manager telling her that the section he was working in were very unhappy with their boss because he was incompetent. He would also tell people in other sections of the company that his boss was having marriage problems (which was not true) and this was interfering with his work performance. When confronted by his boss about this, Wayne convinced him that he had absolutely nothing to do with the misinformation campaign.

Once Wayne was promoted, he had no more time for the people he used to work with, including his old boss. His former colleagues realised that they had been manipulated and started to tell other people in the company about Wayne. Unfortunately, Wayne had already laid the groundwork for his colleagues' dismissal when he previously described them as incompetent and lazy. Now that he was senior to them, he did all he could to have them removed from the company. He gave them unachievable tasks, setting them up for failure, until one by one they were either transferred to other sections of the company or they resigned. None of them was ever promoted while Wayne worked in the company, regardless of their ability. Wayne was extremely proud of this, for him it confirmed his position of absolute power over his former colleagues.

Wayne deliberately cultivated relationships with employees in positions of power and influence, as well as those who could help him advance his career further or make his life easier (for example, he told me it was absolutely vital to be very close to the personal assistant to the director as it allowed him to schedule an appointment to see the powerbrokers of the company whenever he needed to). The cycle of abusing and humiliating those who worked for him, manipulating those at his level and charming those in a position to promote him, eventually resulted in his being made a senior partner in the relatively short period of eight years. What is perhaps most interesting is that once people in the company had no power or influence over Wayne's career, they went from believing they were his friends to knowing they were his victims, and Wayne had engineered the situation so there was absolutely nothing they could do about it. By the time they realised, he was usually their boss. They could only sit back and watch his meteoric rise continue, frustrated by their impotence to intervene.

Once Wayne was made a senior partner, he was able to act out numerous sexually predatory behaviours with his employees. One of his responsibilities after being made a senior partner was to employ staff for a specific section of the company. The positions being filled were were largely junior administrative roles, and Wayne would ensure that he personally interviewed each applicant for a position. He selected his victims from this specially recruited pool of young, naïve employees. Without exception, job applicants who reached the interview stage were female, and Wayne looked for vulnerability and weakness. He was extremely good at detecting attractive, young and inexperienced women who were vulnerable, in much the same way as an African lion is able to rapidly select the weakest member from a herd of antelope and then move in for the kill.

His female victims were vulnerable in different ways. Some felt unattractive, and Wayne would play on this to sexually exploit them, reassuring them and proving to them they were attractive because 'he' was prepared to have sex with them. Others were shy and inexperienced. Wayne took them on 'business' trips. Alone and apprehensive, and frightened that they would lose their jobs if they did not do exactly what he wanted, Wayne coerced them into having sex with him. Wayne's preferred sexual partners were from the shy and inexperienced group of women because afterward they were too ashamed to report what had happened. He also said that they were the easiest group to perform 'unusual' sexual acts with, his sexually sadistic dominance-related behaviours fulfilling his need for absolute control over people.

He easily manipulated a third group of female employees by promising them that if they had a sexual relationship with him they would be promoted. Obviously the promised promotion never materialised. Wayne would invariably tire of the same girl and make life so difficult for her that she would resign, allowing him employ another woman to take her place. Wayne told me that he had lost count of the number of employees he had enjoyed sexual relationships with. Of a group of thirty female ex-employees from this particular section, I found sixteen women who acknowledged they were either coerced or tricked into having sex with Wayne and then resigned from their jobs. It is important at this point to mention that Wayne was married (for the second time) with two children. He had divorced his first wife because she did not understand his need to share himself around. In reality, his first wife left him because she finally tired of the physical, sexual and psychological abuse in the relationship. Wayne married a submissive second wife who was more easily controlled.

Wayne's victims reported feeling as though they had lost control over their lives. Panic attacks, depression, disturbed sleep and nightmares, relationship problems, confusion, disbelief, guilt, lack of trust, anger, powerlessness, flashbacks, shame, embarrassment and sexual dysfunction were only some of the symptoms reported by different victims. Many who had resigned described being unable to look for another job because they could not trust people any more. Others had lost all confidence in their ability to do their jobs. Those employees who chose to stay felt resentment toward a company to whom they had given so much; they believed it had let them down by not listening to or protecting them. The senior partners were also quite disillusioned when they discovered the extent of Wayne's duplicity because they had not been able to detect this psychopath earlier. Instead they realised that they had actually promoted him to a very senior position within the company and then had to devise a strategy to make him disappear from both the company and their lives. They now realised that they had actually allowed a psychopath to flourish.

Around this time the senior partners had started to receive serious complaints from their clients, who were threatening to take their business elsewhere because of unfulfilled promises made by Wayne. These clients were also unhappy about Wayne's arrogant and overbearing manner when they confronted him about unfinished or unsatisfactory work. After paying one large out-of-court settlement to one of Wayne's ex-employees, the company now feared being sued by others, and this was probably another factor that prompted the company to recognise a major problem existed. However, they had absolutely no idea how to eliminate this 'problem' without causing severe harm to the business. There were still some clients who believed in Wayne and refused to do business unless it was with either him or someone he recommended from the company. He did pose a genuine danger to the survival of the company if he was dismissed.

It was at this point that the ability to profile a psychopath such as Wayne was crucial for developing an effective solution to this potentially massive problem for the company. In formulating a strategy for the company, I felt it was crucial to consider the key features of Wayne's personality. First, his egocentric, grandiose belief that he was able to do anything he set his mind to with absolute success, and second, his constant need for excitement and stimulation combined with a lack of responsibility and long-term planning ability. In essence, Wayne was susceptible to an appeal to his ego, and the more exciting the appeal the better because Wayne was not concerned with his long-term future, he was a 'here and now' type of person.

It was decided by the senior partners that Wayne would be informed that he had been specifically selected by the board to develop an Internet business allied with the original company. In fact, he was given the choice of developing the Internet side of the company through the firm, or using his equity in the company to become independent. The board of directors told him that he was an extremely talented partner, and that they believed he was being held back by the limitations of the firm, therefore they were giving him the choice of being stifled by a company that did not really understand him versus an exciting new venture in which he would have complete control over everything and be guaranteed business from the original firm for his first year of operation.

This appeal to Wayne's ego combined with his desire for absolute control over everything in a new company was fanned by the flames of his misguided beliefs about his abilities and the potential for success. I judged that it was almost certain Wayne would choose to leave the company. Of course, if he did leave, it was stipulated that there would also be a transition period in which Wayne would train a new person in how to be as successful as Wayne himself was in handling clients (appealing to his grandiose sense of self-importance). This ensured that Wayne would voluntarily hand over all of his clients, causing minimal if any loss to the firm as Wayne had threatened.

As expected, Wayne decided to leave the company with the large sum of money offered and attempted to start his own dot.com enterprise. The original firm honoured their agreement, passing on a great deal of business to Wayne's new company. True to form, Wayne promised the world to his new clients, but what he delivered fell far short, and with few staff to cover for his ineptitude, his dot.com company collapsed after only six months. Wayne blamed the inability of his staff for the collapse of the business.

The last I heard, Wayne was working in another company, in a senior role, managing a different group of employees, and presumably causing the same untold grief all over again. Interestingly, the company operates in a very different market to the one he worked in previously.

2

DEFINING THE MONSTER — MAD, BAD OR EVIL?

As a GENERAL PATTERN, psychopaths show a distinct cluster of personality characteristics, as well as anti-social behaviours. These characteristics and behaviours include such things as a lack of remorse or guilt, criminal behaviour, an impersonal sex life, impulsive behaviour, lack of responsibility, prolific lying and deception, manipulation of other people to get what they want, apparent lack of conscience, a constant need for stimulation and excitement, superficial charm and good intelligence, unreliability, insincerity, anti-social behaviour, poor judgment and failure to learn by experience, a grandiose sense of their own self-worth, egocentric, an incapacity for love, lack of emotion, absence of life goals, and a chequered employment history. Not all psychopaths will have all of the above characteristics. Different types of psychopaths will have different patterns or 'clusters' of these behaviours.

Sometimes the psychopath is portrayed as being so different from 'normal' people that it is easy to forget they live amongst us. They share our roads, shop where we do and eat at the same restaurants. They also need money, and while some of them get this through criminal behaviours, many of them have jobs, working right alongside us. Despite all the media coverage that highlights the increase of psychopath-related crimes, there is no significant increase. Psychopaths have always lived amongst us.

Most, if not all, people have come across a psychopath at some stage in their lives. Whether they realised that person was a psychopath is a different question entirely.

Are they really out there?

It is estimated that between 1 and 3 adult males in 100 and 1 in every 200 adult females are psychopaths. This means that in a city the size of Sydney, there may be as many as 90,000 male psychopaths and 30,000 female psychopaths. According to Dr Robert Hare, a conservative estimate of the number of psychopaths in North America is about 2 million. In Britain, the number of psychopaths is estimated at 1 in 200 people, a more conservative figure than the American or Australian rates. No research has been definitive about why more males than females are psychopaths.

To be classified as a psychopath, a person must be over the age of eighteen. This is because psychopathy is a personality disorder, or a persistent and repetitive maladaptive way of coping with life. It is certainly possible to have a child who displays antisocial behaviours similar to the psychopath, but a child's personality is not necessarily stable until they reach adulthood. Therefore a psychopath can only be diagnosed in adulthood.

Psychopaths, sociopaths and antisocial personality disorder – are they all the same?

The terms psychopath, sociopath and antisocial personality disorder are often incorrectly used. Each of these terms describes the same general pattern of behaviour, but each label has subtle and important differences concerning cause and diagnosis. Clinicians and researchers who believe that social factors are exclusively responsible for the pattern of behaviours demonstrated by the individual use the term sociopath. Antisocial personality disorder is a term used in the *Diagnostic and Statistical Manual of Mental Disorders*, 4th edition (Revised), used by mental health professionals to describe a persistent, maladaptive behavioural pattern that occurs across the life span. Psychopath, on the other hand, refers to a syndrome of personality and behavioural characteristics. The term psychopath also suggests that the syndrome is caused by psychological, biological, genetic and social factors rather than social factors alone.

Werewolves and dictators – psychopaths throughout history

Psychopaths have always been around, wherever there has been civilisation. A look at the decadent first century Roman emperors, most notably Caligula, reveals how these rulers used their absolute power to seduce their victims and then commit violent and/or sexual acts that usually ended in murder.

Nero, Genghis Khan, Hitler and Stalin are just a few examples of psychopaths who had control over vast empires, causing untold suffering and misery for countless people. It seems that politics, with the inherent power it brings, has always attracted and continues to attract a small group of psychopathic individuals who use this power to satisfy their own needs at the expense of the community. We need look no further than modern day dictators in Africa, or the past dictatorships in Iraq and Serbia for recent examples.

Psychopaths who did not hold positions of power in the societies in which they lived were given a more mythological status. The psychopath as mythological beast was based upon a folk psychology belief that a 'normal' human being could not have performed such 'evil' behaviour, that these people could not be wholly human. Sometimes psychopaths were considered to be part animal or were thought to have supernatural powers. For example, the belief in Lycanthropy, or the transformation of persons into werewolves or some other non-human animal, can be traced back to at least 600 BC when King Nebuchadnezzar believed he suffered from such an affliction. These wolf-like human beings were individuals who literally tore apart their victims, the very same victims they worked alongside, often in the same or neighbouring villages. For example in the 1700s:

> *The corpse of an elderly female was found in rural France. The corpse bore various wounds, some remarkable for their length; the abdomen was ripped open, parts of the intestines were cut out, so was one of the ovaries, other parts were strewn around about the corpse. Several of the wounds were like crosses while one was shaped like a crescent.*

To make sense of this violent murder and playing on superstitions and belief in the mysterious, this woman was seen as the victim of a werewolf. In reality, the unfortunate woman was most likely killed by a psychopath who probably lived and worked in the same village as she did.

Not all psychopaths in history have displayed such extreme violence. For every violent psychopath there have been others who appeared to be 'normal' members of society. One example is recounted by Richard von Krafft-Ebing in *Psychopathia Sexualis* (1886):

> *A sixty-year-old man, Francois, owner of several millions, happily married, father of two daugh-ters, was accustomed to go to the house of a 'procuress' where he was known as the 'prick man' because he would stick one hundred needles*

into a girl's body, fasten with twenty needles a handkerchief upon her bosom, whip the girl, tear the hair from her mons veneris, and squeeze her breasts, etc. When detected, he at first denied the facts, but when convicted expressed his surprise that such a fuss should be made over a mere trifle.

Francois' wife and the community in which he lived had no idea about these psychopathic behaviours being performed by the man they loved and saw as a colleague, a father and a husband. Francois experienced no remorse for his behaviours which indicates he had no conscience. For centuries these psychopathic individuals have been able to hide themselves, chameleon-like, within the fabric of society.

In contemporary times, we are more aware that psychopathy is a personality disorder, or a mental illness, as opposed to some supernatural force. Research is continually being done looking at the causes and different manifestations of psychopathy. Despite a growing understanding of psychopathy by psychologists and the medical profession, which dispels the notion of 'werewolves', the media continue to portray the psychopath as some form of monster. Violent and bizarre criminals, such as Jeffrey Dahmer (dubbed the Milwaukee Monster), are commonly held up as examples of psychopaths in society.

The psychopath – fact versus fiction

There are few more emotive words than 'psychopath' in the English language. Most people immediately think of psychopaths as being serial killers or sexual predators, terrorists and 'hardened' career criminals. Australian serial killers such as Ivan Milat (the Backpacker Murderer), William 'The Mutilator' McDonald, John Glover (the Granny Killer), and international 'monsters' including serial killers Ted Bundy, Jeffrey Dahmer, Dennis Neilsen and Fred and Rose West to name a few, have all been portrayed as quintessential psychopaths. In general, the media tends to focus on sensational acts of extreme violence and then associates this violence with psychopathy. What the media do not portray are the accounts of psychopaths who harm their victims in non-violent ways. This almost exclusive focus on violent criminals as psychopaths perpetuates a misleading belief; that to be a psychopath one must be a physically violent person prepared to perform some physical atrocity on another human being. In reality the non-violent psychopath can be just as devastating, and they are far more common than the 'extreme' serial killers.

Fiction writers also contribute to the myth of psychopaths being unfathomable monsters. In *The Silence of the Lambs* the character of Hannibal Lecter, a serial killer with a penchant for human flesh, is portrayed as the ultimate predator, a 'pure sociopath, impenetrable and too sophisticated for the standard tests'. Television programs such as *Cracker* and *Profiler*, and movies such as *Copycat*, also focus on violent criminals as being psychopaths. While violent criminal psychopaths unquestionably exist, they are a minority of the psychopath population. The images and stereotypes of psychopaths that we are given by the media is the contemporary equivalent of the belief in werewolves. We might think that the serial killer or rapist is terrifying and unpredictable, but it is the psychopath in our workplace who threatens our personal and psychological safety, who is far more common than we are lead to believe.

The psychopath – the reality

The clinical term psychopath (which literally means disease, *pathos*, of the mind, *psyche*) refers to a condition that has only recently begun to be properly described. The psychopath is different from the 'normal' person in a number of ways. The most important difference is the psychopath does not have a conscience. They do not feel any remorse for their behaviours, no matter what devastation they cause in other people's lives. This is because they do not have the ability to empathise with other people. The psychopath is only concerned with how his or her actions will affect their own wellbeing. Detective Sergeant Dennis O'Toole, one of the police officers who arrested Granny Killer John Glover, said 'Glover can and frequently does describe each of his killings in lurid detail, without remorse or emotion'. Detective Inspector Paul Jacob, another policeman who interviewed John Glover commented that 'he talked in a matter of fact way, and spoke of the murders and his actions as if what he had done was as normal as selling a pie'. Glover's biggest regret with regard to brutally killing and then degrading six elderly women is that he will never see his daughters or the ocean again.

Many psychopaths actually get their pleasure or satisfaction from the pain and suffering they cause, deliberately seeking to manipulate and dominate and control those around them. An influential psychiatrist, Dr Hervey Cleckley, wrote in *The Mask of Sanity*: 'goodness, evil, love, horror and humour have no actual meaning, no power to move the psychopath. He is furthermore lacking in the ability to see that others are moved. It is as though he were colour-blind, despite his sharp intelligence, to the emotional aspect of human existence' (p. 90).

Another key difference is that the psychopath experiences emotion differently to other people. They only experience what are known as primary or basic emotions – anger, sadness or distress, excitement and basic fear – shades of grey such as guilt, love and compassion are unfelt. The psychopath does not experience fear in the same way as other people. In a famous experiment conducted in the U.S. during the 1970s, Dr David Lykken tested whether punishment changed psychopaths' behaviour. Psychopaths and a group of non-psychopaths were repeatedly exposed to a sound that was immediately followed by a painful (but non-harmful) electric shock. The non-psychopath group showed high levels of anxiety or tension (measured by the galvanic skin response, the amount of sweat produced on the skin) after hearing the sound as they feared the electric shock they knew was coming. The psychopaths displayed only very limited or no fear after hearing the sound. The knowledge that they were going to experience a painful shock after hearing the sound produced only a moderate and very brief fear response. In other words, the psychopaths did not have the same fear of negative events or consequences as the non-psychopaths.

Dr Robert Hare performed a similar experiment in which he also observed that psychopaths showed fewer signs of this 'anticipatory fear' than non-psychopaths. This is important because fear motivates people not to do certain things. For the psychopath, they are more likely to perform a negative behaviour, even though they know it will have unpleasant consequences. They think in the 'here and now' as opposed to longer term, and their control over their impulses is usually impaired or non-existent.

The psychopath may also be impulsive. Things are done with little regard for consequences. Often the psychopath will say that 'the time was right', they 'felt like it', they 'could not stop themselves', they 'had to do it', etc. They do not always consider the negative aspects associated with their impulsive behaviours. The psychopath rarely thinks they will be caught for doing the wrong thing. However, this characteristic is not unique to the psychopath.

Psychologists have observed a phenomenon known as optimism bias, in which people generally believe that a risk to themselves is lower than the risk for the rest of the population. For example, many people think that other people are more likely to get skin cancer, have heart attacks, be mugged, have car accidents, have their house burn down, etc, than they are. In other words, people believe that a negative event is more likely to happen to someone else rather than to them. If you have ever exceeded the speed limit while driving, did you think you would be caught or have an accident? Most likely you thought that everything would be okay. Psychopaths do not think about being caught either.

Simon is one example of a psychopath who was impulsive.

Simon, a diagnosed psychopath, was a very successful businessman. He owned a powerful performance car that he used to drive at extremely high speeds (he boasted that he drove 120-140 km/ph in 50 km/ph zones), regardless of the danger he placed himself or other people in. He simply did not think of the consequences. He knew that he could lose his licence or kill someone but said this did not bother him at all; he would rather 'live life to the full' than be imprisoned by rules. Simon was killed a few years ago when he had a collision with another car. Simon was aware of the potential consequences for his behaviour, he simply did not care.

One interesting experiment done on psychopaths in the 1970s showed that some learning is possible, if the consequences for their behaviour are important to the psychopath. An American researcher trained three groups of people (non-psychopaths, criminals who were not psychopaths, and criminal psychopaths) to perform a specific behaviour in order to avoid experiencing a negative event (for example, to avoid receiving an electric shock a person may have to press a button). There were three possible negative events; an electric shock (physical punishment), the experimenter would say 'wrong' (social punishment), and loss of money (the experimenter would take away some money that had been given to the subjects for every incorrect response).

Non-psychopathic subjects learned the behaviour very well in the face of all three negative events. Non-psychopathic criminals (people convicted of criminal offences who are not psychopaths) did not care about the social punishment, but learned quickly when money was taken or when they were physically punished. The psychopaths only responded when the negative event involved the confiscation of their money. They did not respond to physical or social punishment.

From these observations it seems that psychopaths are perfectly capable of learning to do specific behaviours, but social and physical punishments have little effect on their behaviour. It seems that removing something of value to the psychopath can be an effective tool for controlling their behaviour. Instead of fearing punishment, the psychopath may in fact be hypersensitive to rewards, leading to a variety of anti-social or ruthless behaviours to obtain these rewards (or to prevent rewards, such as money, from being taken away).

Psychopaths also process information about the world in a different way to the rest of the population. Psychologists have noticed that as well as displaying less fear than other people; the psychopath also pays less attention to disturbing or upsetting emotionally 'charged' words. For example, if I were to show you the words 'rape' or 'murder', you would most likely pay more attention than if I were to show you the words 'bicycle' or 'car'. This is because 'rape' and 'murder' are emotionally charged negative words that are very unpleasant; people unconsciously pay more attention to them. The psychopath, on the other hand, would process 'murder' or 'rape' at the same level as 'car' or 'bicycle'. The brain activity of the psychopath does not change when exposed to the emotional words, which is in contrast to non-psychopaths, who display greater brain activity for the emotional words. Consider the following case:

> Ben noticed a crowd of people had gathered on a crowded railway station, all intently looking down at something on the tracks. He walked over and saw that some of the people in the crowd were crying, and then noticed a mangled body lying on the tracks below. Ben could not understand why the people were crying. He did not feel anything, apart from being annoyed when he realised that he would be significantly delayed while they 'cleaned up the mess'. Ben saw the people who were crying as weak, and it just confirmed for him that he was right to loathe society.

The psychopath quite often makes broad generalisations about the world, thinking in absolute terms. Psychopaths evaluate and justify their behaviours using these generalised beliefs as a reference point.

For example, many psychopaths justify their behaviour by saying that all people are out to survive any way that they can, and anyone else in their position would have done exactly the same thing.

Tim was in therapy for anger management problems. He displayed (amongst many other things) impulsive and violent outbursts. One of his many offences involved punching a woman in a supermarket checkout queue. Tim believed that people were against him; constantly trying to dominate him (probably because he tried to dominate everyone around him) and that this 'bitch' had deliberately pushed her trolley into his ankle while he was waiting in the queue. He said that he punched her in the face because he had to show her who was boss. Tim felt the need to execute a completely inappropriate behaviour based upon his inaccurate belief that everyone was out to get him. Tim said he would act exactly the same if the situation happened again. Why?

In Tim's mind, punching the woman worked; everyone in the supermarket saw not to mess with him, and the woman who was lying injured on the floor was certainly not going to mess with him again. He did say that he was sorry for what he did, as he had to go to court, and was given a custodial sentence. When I asked him what he thought the victim would be feeling, he told me that life was tough and it was everyone for themselves, he had no time to think about what she was feeling because he had enough problems of his own.

Psychopaths are generally grandiose and filled with a narcissistic sense of self-importance. They commonly overestimate their abilities and inflate their accomplishments, often appearing boastful or pretentious. Quite often they will attribute blame for negative things that happen to them (such as going to court, being declared bankrupt, etc) to factors beyond their control, such as bad luck or 'getting a raw deal'. They often intend to pursue a career with status and authority, as opposed to some form of 'hands on' work that they believe is beneath them. It is useful to ask the psychopath their opinion of other people, as they frequently see them as stupid, boring, mindless, etc. Again, this shows the psychopath's belief in their superiority over other people. Note that while many people display this superiority toward other people, the majority of them are not psychopaths.

The psychopath is often sexually promiscuous. Sexual relations are characterised by impersonal affairs, one night stands, multiple sexual partners, infidelity, use of prostitutes, participation in a wide variety of sexual 'scenes' (bondage, S&M, etc). They may also coerce their victims into having sexual relations by promising to promote them, playing on a psychological vulnerability, or by conning naïve, inexperienced partners. The psychopath generally feels little or no emotional attachment to sexual partners, they are seen as vehicles to be used for sexual gratification. Responsibility is rarely taken for any children that are the result of their frequent sexual liaisons. Most commonly the psychopath is proud of their sexual prowess, as they feel it validates them as a powerful person.

A question I'm often asked concerns how the psychopath is able to convince numerous women or men to have sex with them. There are a number of strategies the psychopath will use to have sex with willing partners. These are presented in the box below. It should be noted that the sexual strategies do not indicate psychopathy in and of themselves, they are simply some techniques used by psychopaths (and some non-psychopaths) to get what they want sexually from a 'voluntary' partner.

Sexual strategies used by the psychopath

- Verbally or physically threaten partner.

- Suggest limiting sexual interaction on first date and then insisting on full intercourse.

- Using alcohol or drugs to loosen partner's inhibitions about sex.

- Flatter partner and drop hints that they want to have sex.

- Insult or ridicule partner until they comply.

- Act helpless so partner feels sorry for them.

- Sulk when told not having sex until partner relents.

- Remind partner of favours done in the past for them.

- Use props such as pretending they are a policeman, important person, celebrity, etc.

- Act cold toward partner until they finally give in and have sex.

- Do something special for partner so they 'owe' sex to the psychopath.

- Tell partner how much they love them and put self physically close to partner.

- Assert their authority over their partner.

- Become angry with partner until partner complies with sexual demands.

Nature or nurture?

There is some controversy about whether a psychopath is created by nature (born) or nurture (environment), or a combination of the two. The idea that it is a combination of genes, biology and the environment that produce the psychopathy syndrome has a great deal of resonance.

All in the head?

The brain is an infinitely complex organ, one of the last unexplored frontiers in science. To understand the brain, and how it functions, it is necessary to understand how billions of cells all function and interact with each other at the same time. Neurologists divide the brain into four sections, or 'lobes'. Each lobe plays a different role in regulating our behaviour.

It has been well established that one of these sections, known as the frontal lobe, plays a crucial role in regulating social behaviour. Where the frontal lobe is not functioning as it should be, maladaptive social behaviour characterised by persistent violations of social conventions and moral rules may occur. Impaired frontal lobe functioning can also result in impulsive and/or inappropriate behaviour. One group of American researchers found that male psychopaths have less grey and white brain matter in the pre-frontal lobe (a part of the frontal lobe) when compared with normal men (Raine et al., 2000). These researchers found that there was less brain activity in the pre-frontal region of the frontal lobe in the male psychopaths.

Another region of the brain that has been identified as being different in the psychopath is the amygdala, which is part of the brain's limbic system, located almost in the centre of the brain. It is very important in regulating emotion and, in particular, it is crucial for learning and remembering emotionally significant events. It generates fear, which then initiates a fight or flight response. James Blair, a researcher at the University College, London, has observed that the amygdala functions differently in the psychopath when compared with the non-psychopath. In other experiments conducted using rats, it was found that when the amygdala was lesioned (or destroyed), the rats no longer learned fear responses, that is, the rats no longer avoided a stimulus they had previously associated with pain.

The brain functions as a system, and the interaction between various parts of the brain is also an extremely important factor to consider. Just looking at one part of the brain as the 'cause' of psychopathy may result in another equally important component in a different section of the brain to be missed. For example, research is emerging which suggests the temporal lobe (broadly responsible for language, self-esteem and perceptions of self-identity) and the various connections or pathways between different regions of the brain may also be extremely important in shaping the psychopath's behaviour.

It is tempting to look at the differences in psychopaths' brains and conclude that because their brains are different they must have been born that way, and therefore they have no control over their behaviours. This is not entirely accurate for two reasons.

First, we do not know if the psychopath was born with brain abnormalities, or whether the abnormalities developed over time as the psychopath matured and experienced different life events. It is impossible to determine which possibility is true, because it would be unethical to let a child with these abnormalities grow up into a psychopath, and it would be equally unethical to destroy these parts of an adult brain to see if the person becomes a psychopath.

Second, the distinction between the biological brain and the philosophical concept of the mind has not been resolved. For example, if you and I experience exactly the same event (say, watching a movie) it theoretically activates the same visual areas of our brains. This does not explain why each of us remembers different aspects of the movie, nor does it explain why you enjoyed the movie and I wish I saw a different one. It is our subjective experiences that shape our different interpretations of the world, despite having biologically similar brains and neural responses.

All in the genes?

Family, twin and adoption studies all suggest genes may have an influence on psychopathy. Studies have found that where a child has a criminal parent, the child is more likely to become a criminal. For example, one study looked at children born to criminals who were adopted by non-criminal families versus children born to non-criminals adopted by normal families. The children who had criminal parents were more likely to become criminals and have antisocial personalities, despite being raised in a non-criminal family environment. Twin studies also tend to support the importance of genes in subsequent criminality. Of identical twins, in 55 per cent of the cases where one identical twin performed criminal behaviour the other identical twin also performed criminal behaviour. In non-identical twins, only 13 per cent of twins were both criminals.

In looking at the role of genes on psychopathy, and on criminality in general, there are a number of important factors to consider. Not all criminals are psychopaths, which limits the relevance of some research studies to psychopathy, particularly where researchers only looked at criminality. Another factor is that using twins is problematic where they are raised in the same family, as they may also share similar environments that contributed to their anti-social behaviours. It also needs to be considered that genetic factors cannot be 100 per cent responsible for antisocial behaviour. While genes play some role in antisocial behaviour and most likely psychopathy as well, it is clear that the environment also contributes significantly.

It is likely that a genetic predisposition exists for psychopathy, and to become a psychopath it is also necessary to be exposed to a particular type of environment. Genetic factors may contribute to the development of psychopathic behaviour only in the presence of certain environmental factors.

All in the upbringing?

A number of environmental factors play a role in the development of the psychopath. Often we hear that people who perform psychopathic behaviours have been either physically or sexually abused as children, and this has caused them to become the people they are. While this may be a compelling argument, it does not explain why most people who are physically or sexually abused do not go on to become psychopaths.

The effect of environmental factors on the develop-ment of the psychopath is more complex than it first seems. Given that a number of different types of psychopaths exist (organisational psychopath, corporate criminal psychopath, violent criminal psychopath, and occupational psychopath) it seems logical that growing up in different environments leads to different types of psychopaths. While subtle differences exist, there are some environmental elements common to all psychopaths.

The first and perhaps most important environmental factor experienced in development is not one specific event. What is important is how the psychopath experiences or sees a number of events in their lives. The social environment in which the child develops has the most influence on how the psychopath interprets their world. Studies looking at violent criminal psychopaths have found that poor social environments lead to deviant behaviours and thought patterns from a very early age. For example, if a child's parents ignore their child's behaviours, the child learns early on that there are no consequences for the behaviour. They also learn that the only person who is going to protect and take care of them is themselves.

Where a person is rewarded frequently for a behaviour, the behaviour will be repeated, just like when you give a dog a treat every time it sits when commanded, eventually the dog will sit on command. For the developing psychopath, if they receive money for conning someone, or feel good after bullying another person, these behaviours will be repeated. If the child performs behaviours that make them feel good and powerful, such as stealing lollies from the corner store, the only thing the child is thinking is that if they steal things they want it makes them feel good, therefore they will do it again. Not only will the behaviours be repeated, they will be expanded upon. For example, the behaviours may evolve from conning other children to shoplifting and finally to stealing from the company they work for. The developing psychopath will accept these behaviours as a way of living and the pattern is set for future behaviour.

Quite often, when a child's parents ignore them, other things are also present in the family environment. In a study I conducted looking at sexual homicide offenders in 2001, it emerged that many had been exposed to criminal behaviours (stealing property, sexual assault, animal cruelty, etc) and had witnessed domestic violence between parents. This provided an example or role model for these children, teaching them how to resolve conflict (with violence) as well as providing a model for how to feel powerful and in control (by being violent toward other people). For the young psychopath, a lot of their antisocial behaviours are learned from deviant models in their life. For example, a child growing up where domestic violence is present learns how to dominate another person by modelling the behaviour of the abusive parent.

Television can also provide deviant models, with increasing levels of gratuitous violence and crime being watched by younger and younger children. Where appropriate parental guidance is not present, younger children may consider what they witness on television as socially normal. Often this is displayed in play patterns, which may be hostile and aggressive. I am not saying that television makes psychopaths; I am suggesting that it desensitises some children to particular behaviours. When this desensitisation is combined with the other biological and environmental factors already mentioned, prolonged antisocial behaviour patterns may develop and continue throughout the life span. This cognitive-behavioural pattern becomes quite powerful later in life. Combined with the feeling that society's rules do not apply to them, it can lead to extreme forms of violence toward other people with no feeling of remorse. This ambivalence or apathy toward society and its values is referred to as negative social attachment.

In the case of a child who has loving and devoted parents, psychopathic behaviour can still develop. Some psychopaths I have interviewed who came from 'normal' families described feeling smothered by their parents, as though they had no control over what they were allowed to do. What is important here is the child's perception of their social environment, rather than the reality of the actual environment. Where one feels smothered by a parent, the reaction may be the same as for a child who grew up in a non-caring family environment: both children seek control over their own lives. One psychopath told me:

> *My mother was always telling me what to do, everything I did was wrong, and I hated her for it. I was never good enough. Things always had to be done her way, in her time. People looked at my family and could not understand how*

*I became what I am now. Well, eventually I just
thought fuck it, I can't do anything right anyway,
so I might as well do whatever the hell I want
because I am going to get the same crap from her
anyway.*

In the presence of an environment in which a child
feels they have no control over their lives, certain
thought processes and related behaviours develop.
Often these children feel powerless and a sense of
being different from other people. They see no reason
for following the rules when they get what they want
by breaking them. They may be rebellious, aggressive,
frequent liars, and feel entitled to whatever they want
in life.

Children who bully others are often socially
isolated and don't always develop a good understanding of social rules or acceptable behaviours. This is
because the children they bully never fully accept them
socially. The bully's relationships are based on fear
rather than friendship. The bully may then interpret
fear as a basis for all relationships, and this becomes a
normal part of the relationships they form. In other
words, they get what they want from other people
through fear and intimidation.

Not all psychopaths were bullies as children. Some
of them may have been passive, shaping themselves
to fit in with other people's wishes, blending in with
their surroundings. Often these children are the 'quiet
manipulators' who achieve their goals at the expense of
others without their victims even noticing something

was wrong until it was too late. Later in life these children are more likely to engage in non-confrontational, non-violent antisocial behaviours such as quietly defrauding a company of millions.

As the child becomes older, they engage in more antisocial behaviours. They are also more likely to be caught doing the wrong thing by people outside of their families. This is where the young psychopath compares consequences with rewards gained from doing the wrong thing. One example that stands out for me is a case of a fourteen-year-old boy who stole a high performance car and was chased by the police a number of times on the same night before being caught. When he was finally apprehended, the teenager was brought to the police station and spoken to by police about his behaviour, which he thought was quite amusing. The police emphasised to his parents that this was a serious offence, and when he went home with his parents they told him how stupid he was for being caught and that was the end of the matter. From the young offender's viewpoint, the extreme excitement and adrenalin rush of stealing the car and being chased by the police was far greater than the consequences of being given no real punishment from either the police or his parents. It is highly likely that he would continue to steal cars and drive in a manner that could possibly kill an innocent person. This young man was later arrested for stealing high performance cars to order for a car-rebirthing ring.

When looking at the role of environment on the development of psychopathy, it is easy to look back over the life of a psychopath and select events that seem likely to have caused the person to become a psychopath. What is important to look at is how many children experience negative environments and do not go on to become psychopaths. For example, not all children who are abused become psychopaths. I believe it is the unique combination of biological, genetic and environmental factors that interact in a specific way to produce a psychopath. Researchers and clinicians are still looking at the exact nature of this interaction.

Identifying psychopaths
Behind the mask of sanity

One of the most influential clinicians to research psychopathy was an American forensic psychiatrist, Dr Hervey Cleckley. In 1941 he published a classic book called *The Mask of Sanity*, in which he declared that psychopaths were a significant but largely ignored problem in society. In detailed case studies, Cleckley described patients he had seen, providing the first glimpse into the world of the psychopath. Cleckley claimed that the psychopath was living behind a mask of sanity, appearing to the casual observer to be the same as anyone else. He identified a constellation of sixteen major characteristics of the psychopath, which are sometimes referred to as the Cleckley criteria for psychopathy.

Cleckley's list of characteristics provides a good picture of what most psychopaths are like. They are unconcerned for other people's feelings and suffer no

Cleckley psychopathy criteria

Note: *The characteristics listed below cannot be used to diagnose yourself or anybody else as a psychopath.*

1. Superficial charm and good intelligence.
2. Absence of delusions and other signs of irrational thinking.
3. Absence of nervousness and other psychoneurotic manifestations.
4. Unreliability.
5. Untruthfulness and insincerity.
6. Lack of remorse or shame.
7. Inadequately motivated antisocial behaviour.
8. Poor judgment and failure to learn by social experience.
9. Pathologic egocentricity and incapacity for love.
10. General poverty in major affective (emotional) reactions.
11. Specific loss of insight.
12. Unresponsiveness in interpersonal relations.
13. Fantastic and uninviting behaviour.
14. Suicide rarely carried out.
15. Sex life impersonal, trivial and poorly integrated.
16. Failure to follow any life plan.

remorse or guilt if their actions hurt others. Although they may be superficially charming, they do not form real friendships; they often become con artists or confidence tricksters. Both male and female psychopaths may be sexually promiscuous from an early age, but these encounters do not seem to mean much to them. They tend to be unfaithful to their partners, and separations and divorce (if they married in the first place) are common.

Psychopaths do not easily learn from negative experiences and tend to repeat behaviours that get them into trouble. Psychopaths habitually tell lies, even when there is no apparent reason for doing so. Paul Ekman, a well-known researcher looking at deceptive behaviour has termed this 'duping delight'. It seems the psychopath may simply enjoy lying for the sake of lying itself. The psychopath is even likely to lie when the deception may be discovered.

Without conscience – the Psychopathy Checklist (Revised)

Canadian psychologist, Dr Robert Hare, has further advanced knowledge of the psychopath immeasurably over the past thirty years. Building on Cleckley's checklist, Dr Hare developed a standard measurement system that could reliably identify psychopaths. This was called the Psychopathy Checklist (Revised), or the PCL(R), and it is still used today to 'distinguish with reasonable certainty true psychopaths from people who merely break the rules' (Hare 1993, p. 32).

Two important dimensions of the psychopathic

Psychopaths can beat lie detector tests

Lie detector tests do not work on psychopaths. The lie detector test relies on identifying specific bodily responses that occur when a person lies; galvanic skin response (GSR), or sweat produced by the body, and heart rate. The theory is that when a normal person lies, they feel anxious about getting caught, as well as a little guilty about telling the lie itself. When anxiety increases due to the guilt and fear of being caught, GSR and heart rate both increase slightly. The 'lie detector' is sensitive to these physiological changes, and therefore 'detects' when a person is lying as GSR and heart rate are greater than when they are telling the truth. However, the psychopath does not get as anxious as other people in general, and they certainly feel no guilt about lying. Therefore the psychopath's physiological responses are exactly the same when they are lying as when they are telling the truth, and consequently the lie is not 'detected'. The ability to beat a lie detector test cannot be considered an accurate means of identifying a psychopath, as ordinary people can also learn to control their own anxiety responses to 'fool' the test.

personality were identified by Dr Hare – emotional/interpersonal aspects and social deviance. Each of these dimensions, or factors, is made up of specific

Items in the Psychopathy
Checklist (Revised) – PCL(R)

Note: *The characteristics listed below cannot be used to diagnose yourself or anybody else as a psychopath.*

1. Glibness/superficial charm.
2. Grandiose sense of self-worth.
3. Need for excitement.
4. Pathological lying.
5. Conning/manipulative.
6. Lack of remorse or guilt.
7. Shallow affect (emotion).
8. Callous/lack of empathy.
9. Parasitic lifestyle.
10. Poor behavioural controls.
11. Promiscuous sexual behaviour.
12. Early behavioural problems.
13. Lack of realistic, long-term goals.
14. Impulsivity.
15. Irresponsibility.
16. Failure to accept responsibility for actions.
17. Many short-term marital relationships.
18. Juvenile delinquency.
19. Revocation of conditional release.
20. Criminal versatility.

traits that can be identified and scored on the Psychopathy Checklist. However, it is extremely important to note that it is not possible to diagnose a person as a psychopath based on the information in this book. Only appropriately trained and qualified professionals are capable of making a diagnosis of psychopathy.

Dr Hare warns people to 'be aware that people who are *not* psychopaths may have *some* of the symptoms described [in the checklist]. Many people are impulsive, or glib, or cold and unfeeling, or antisocial, but this does not mean they are psychopaths. Psychopathy is a *syndrome* – a cluster of related symptoms'.

The characteristics in the PCL(R) were largely based on studies of people in prison, yet the majority of psychopaths are not necessarily in prison. Chapter 3 looks at the characteristics of psychopaths who have been observed in workplaces across Australia and overseas.

3
PSYCHOPATHS AT WORK – ARE THEY ALL THE SAME?

NOT ALL PSYCHOPATHS are violent criminals. Workplace psychopaths hide behind respectability and fulfil their desires in a variety of ways. While they may be intelligent and cunning, psychopaths in the workplace are not all the same. The characteristics outlined by Professor Hare and Dr Cleckley in Chapter 2 generally apply to the broad outline of the psychopath, but more specific sub-types exist. Psychopaths in the workplace can be classified into four types: the organisational psychopath; the corporate criminal psychopath; the violent criminal psychopath; and the occupational psychopath.

Each psychopath sub-type is characterised by a specific pattern of characteristics, as well as variations in profession and lifestyle. It is important to realise that psychopathic behaviours from each category can overlap, and certain individuals may evolve from one sub-type into another. For example, an occupational psychopath who is a police officer may use his position of authority to harass members of the public, getting satisfaction from his ability to control and manipulate others, feeling absolutely no remorse for his inappropriate use of power. It is conceivable that this same police officer may develop into a serial rapist who uses his position to camouflage and facilitate his sexually predatory behaviours. In short, he could evolve from an occupational psychopath into a violent criminal psychopath. However, just because he has developed into a serial rapist does not mean that he has stopped intimidating motorists because it gives him a sense of power and control over them.

While the categories are not absolute, it is useful to explore each psychopath sub-type to get an insight into the precise impact they have on the workplace.

The organisational psychopath

The organisational psychopath has a number of strategies they use to manipulate their way into the upper levels of the company they work for. They are found in all types of companies, at all levels, from chief executives to workers on the factory floor. There are two objectives for many organisational psychopaths. The first objective is to get to the top for the financial rewards and the power the position brings.

David worked for a large insurance company, and had a variety of techniques and devious strategies that helped him get promoted. Among other things, he would steal co-workers projects so he looked better than they did, he would spread false rumours about his boss, he lied to clients to make sure he got the contract, and then passed the work on to someone else who would get the blame when services were not delivered as he had promised. David was an up-and-coming star in the company. Most people had no idea that he had ruthlessly achieved his numerous promotions at the expense of the people around him.

The second objective is to revel in the suffering and misery they inflict on the people they work with.

Mark was a senior manager of the Australian division of a multi-national company. He had read about my consulting work for companies with 'psychopathic' employees, and organised a meeting, as he wanted to discuss a few things regarding his staff. Mark said that his employees were very unhappy, constantly under stress, and resigning at unprecedented rates. Mark said he knew the cause of this, himself. He had deliberately implemented policies in the company to increase the workload and stress levels because he enjoyed watching people trying to work under more pressure than they could cope with. He wanted me to tell him about the strategies used by psychopaths I had seen so he could try those as well. Needless to say, I was stunned and terminated the meeting immediately. As part of my duty of care to the employees, I also requested a meeting with the Australian managing director and informed him about a potential reason for the company's high staff turnover rate. I believe Mark was transferred to an overseas division of the company for 'career development'.

The organisational psychopath can be the boss, an employee or a co-worker. They use an arsenal of psychological techniques designed to cause as much confusion and conflict as possible within the organisation. Undermining others, character assassination, blackmail, seduction and outright lying are just some of the techniques used to destroy the careers and lives of their co-workers.

A range of common behavioural and personality traits stand out amongst the organisational psychopaths I have observed in the course of my work in corporations.

These characteristics can be listed under the following broad areas.
• Organisational/Managerial Behaviour
• Interpersonal Behaviour
• Emotional/Individual Characteristics

In terms of organisational/managerial conduct, organisational psychopaths often display similar patterns of behaviour. Generally their behaviour disrupts the smooth running of a workplace due to their manipulative strategies and a general disregard for the people they work with. These types can be unpredictable, bullying, lack direction in their work, can't be depended on, and have very low tolerance levels to boredom. Similar characteristics in the Psychopathy Checklist (Revised) in Chapter 2 include parasitic lifestyles, poor behavioural controls, adult antisocial behaviours and

Organisational Psychopath Characteristics

Organisational/ Managerial Behaviour	Interpersonal Behaviour	Emotional/Individual Characteristics
• Manipulative (at an organisational level)	• Manipulative (at an interpersonal level)	• Unfeeling
• Unethical behaviour	• Deceitful/devious/false	• Lacking a conscience
• Intolerant/easily bored	• No responsibility taken for own actions	• Grandiose/self-important
• Unpredictable/shallow emotions	• Intimidating	• Egocentric/narcissistic
• Parasitic behaviour	• Charming/superficial	• Shallow emotions
• Undependable		• Pathological lying
• Bullying (not necessarily confined to work)		• Marital problems
• Seek increased power and control in the company		• Sexual promiscuity
• Create conflict between organisation members		• Impulsive

irresponsibility. Generally the organisational/managerial conduct characteristics are typified by a desire for increased power and control within the company. This often creates conflict between other members of the organisation as they will do whatever it takes to get that power and control. The organisational psychopath takes delight in this conflict, as the atmosphere of confusion and hostility allows them to continue manipulating the situation for their own advantage.

> Anne was a senior executive in a marketing firm. Her behaviour was completely unpredictable. It shifted from looking at a specific contract to criticising her colleagues for no reason. She was impatient about anything that did not interest her, lacked focus for specific jobs (she would delegate to other people after failing to meet her own deadlines) and her co-workers could not rely on anything she said. One of the few things that you could rely on with Anne was that she would let you down somehow, and always avoid being criticised for her irresponsibility. Anne was also renowned for doing whatever it took to 'get the contract', no matter how unethical the behaviour, and then bullying her subordinates into doing the impossible. At the end of the process it always seemed to be Anne who looked good at the expense of everyone else who actually did the work. She had an incredible ability to manipulate any situation so that she always came out looking successful.

The organisational psychopath's interpersonal conduct is marred by a general lack of trustworthiness.

This behaviour is characterised by the common theme of power and control, a complete lack of consideration for other people's feelings, manipulative and intimidating behaviour, deceit, and a devious charm. Interpersonal conduct revolves around serving the interests of the organisational psychopath and any collateral damage caused to other people is either a bonus or of no concern.

Luke was a bully when it came to dealing with his subordinates. He had no insight into how his behaviour made other people feel. He would shout at people, criticise them for his own mistakes, and expect them to do things he knew were unreasonable. He would call them names, intimidate the newer members of his section, and he took delight in ruining the careers of anyone who challenged him. Luke was not trusted by anyone in the office, it was common knowledge that anything he said was to be taken with a grain of salt because he would lie without hesitation. The people who worked for Luke felt trapped, as they needed his 'favourable ratings' for their careers to advance further. Luke took full advantage of the situation.

An unfeeling nature, a grandiose sense of self-worth, lack of remorse or guilt, self-importance, pathological lying, shallow emotions, sexual promiscuity and an impulsive nature are some of the emotional and individual characteristics of the organisational psychopath. The individual and emotional characteristics are the foundation for both the organisational/managerial and interpersonal behaviours. In a sense, the emotional and individual characteristics reflect the personality of each psychopathic sub-type.

The corporate criminal psychopath

The corporate criminal psychopath commits criminal acts through their profession or as part of an organised ring devoted to corporate crime. Their behaviours may be criminal and/or sub-criminal (ethically and/or morally wrong but technically not illegal) to gain a financial or other advantage for themselves at the expense of other people. This category includes bank employees who defraud their employer, stockbrokers involved in scams, builders who 'con' clients, real estate agents who dupe homeowners, lawyers who spend their clients trust funds, second-hand car sales-people who alter cars to get a sale, gangs who are involved in identity theft and the use of fraudulent cheques and so on. The number of schemes and strategies used by the corporate criminal psychopath are limitless; when they are caught they simply work out a new way to continue their criminal behaviours.

Sue was a reliable and trusted worker in the finance industry. People respected her efficiency and pleasant way of dealing with both clients and other staff members. She seemed to be one of the hardest workers in the office, doing lots of overtime late into the night. She had a devoted husband who thought she was a very senior executive at the bank given her large 'salary'. Sue used to make all the mortgage repayments, bought a high performance car with cash, took the family on many overseas holidays, and generally lived a very luxurious lifestyle. No one realised that Sue was transferring large sums of money into accounts she had set up under false names.

It was while Sue was on holiday that her replacement noticed some abnormalities that resulted in an audit and she was subsequently charged with fraud. Sue's co-workers were shocked. On further investigation, it turned out that Sue had used some of the money she stole to finance an affair she was having. She also 'dabbled' in the use of illegal drugs such as cocaine. It was discovered that Sue had a secret past, including convictions for stealing, drink driving, driving whilst disqualified and drug use. Sue expressed no remorse for her crime to her husband or those around her, but she was sorry that she had been caught. To the courts she expressed a great deal of remorse and apologised profusely for her actions, stating that she realised the error of her ways and that it would never happen again, presumably hoping to receive a lighter sentence.

The corporate criminal psychopath is usually glib and superficial, a brilliant con artist who excels at creating exactly the right impression to suit their criminal behaviours. They lie when they need to, and are not intimidated by the possibility of getting caught out. Dr Robert Hare in his book *Without Conscience* has identified that these types change their stories or rework the facts when they are caught out in a lie, which results in a series of contradictory statements and a thoroughly confused listener. Psychologist Paul Ekman has identified that some of the lies serve no purpose, with the motivation simply being the delight associated with duping other people.

You name the subject and Robert could talk about it as though he was an authority on the matter. He could switch from one topic to another, depending on the audience. Robert had been convicted of numerous fraud and deception offences. Robert said he found it easy, and indeed amusing, to figure out what and how to press the right buttons so people were 'tripping over themselves' to give him huge amounts of money. He said that most people were motivated by greed and his 'get rich quick' schemes would never have worked had it not been for people's blindness to common sense when promised massive returns on their investments with little or no effort on their part.

Robert had lengthy discussions with his victims about their goals in life, their dreams and their troubles. He would sympathise with them, and then use this information in the package of lies he presented to them as his 'investment package'. He told people what they wanted to hear. Like Sue, Robert expressed no sympathy for any of his victims, many of whom had lost their life savings in his phony investment schemes.

The corporate criminal psychopath is often intelligent, and has a thorough understanding of the financial arena in which they work their frauds. This is usually combined with a number of the characteristics associated with psychopathy, including a lack of conscience, a grandiose sense of their own self-importance, a willingness to use deceitful and manipulative strategies, a lack of responsibility and a constant need for excitement. For the corporate criminal psychopath, the low probability of detection and relatively light penalties for fraud (for example, twenty-five years for an armed robbery in maximum security compared with ten years for fraud in a minimum security institution), makes non-violently separating people from their money more attractive than committing violent crime.

When corporate criminal psychopaths are identified, a large number use their abilities to avoid responsibility, and therefore punishment for their behaviours. Sunil De Silva, a crown prosecutor for the NSW Department of Public Prosecutions, says these people are well versed in playing the system. 'They use all of their manipulative skills to delay court proceedings, citing all sorts of legal and personal reasons for this. Frustratingly, they are sham artists of the highest order and often get away with it' (Clarke and Shea, 2001, p. 106). When the matter finally does go to trial, quite often they will blame other people in the company, or say that it was a management issue and they did not mean to deceive anybody. If only people had not made a rush on the company funds everything would have been fine and all the 'borrowed' money would have been returned. If they are found guilty, they then claim to be extremely sorry for their behaviour, and 'promise' never to do it again to get the lightest sentence possible. The next step, if these types are convicted, is using their manipulative skills to persuade the parole board to release them as quickly as possible.

It is important to note that the corporate criminal psychopath is not necessarily the person who occasionally steals from their company, or who takes home stationery without permission. The important characteristics of psychopathy are still crucial when evaluating whether someone is psychopathic versus a thief or a liar (remember that not all thieves and liars are psychopaths). The psychopath displays no remorse for their actions, and must have a cluster of psychopathic behaviours, not just one or two.

The violent criminal psychopath

Perhaps the most familiar type of psychopath, as a result of extensive mass media coverage, are those who hold down a job, yet never come to the attention of anyone until they are apprehended for serious violent crimes. The violent criminal psychopath hurts people physically in a range of ways, primarily to feel powerful and in control of themselves. Crimes can include rape, murder, stalking, domestic violence, assault, arson and the entire gamut of violent offences. Often when people think of violent criminals, they only associate the person with the crime committed, ignoring other aspects of the violent criminal psychopath's life.

Greg was a very influential academic at a prestigious university. He was extremely intelligent and well respected in his field, having won numerous research awards and external grants. He frequently did consulting work for both Australian and international firms. Greg was also a paedophile. He used to spend much of his spare time observing and photographing prepubescent boys in public places. When a search warrant was executed at his house and office thousands of child porn pictures and movies were found on his computers. He also kept a journal in which he described having sadistic sex with under-age males. When he was arrested Greg continued to play mind games with the police, never admitting that he had done the wrong thing. He tried to justify paedophilia by saying that it was love and not abuse.

The violent criminal psychopath performs a variety of criminal behaviours, where each particular behaviour reveals something different about them. There are different types of murderers, rapists, paedophiles, stalkers, and arsonists. Not all of these people are psychopaths. Some are mentally ill, others act under the influence of drugs or alcohol, and others become so angry that they lose control. A significant proportion of these violent criminals, particularly those who are recidivist offenders, are psychopaths. Violent criminal psychopaths also perform multiple criminal behaviours, such as car theft, break and enter, malicious damage and drug offences.

Contrary to the sensational media portrayals of these types, they frequently have partners and families. Many work in a range of jobs from police officer to priest, social worker to executive. Some of these sub-type offenders have harmed people they have worked with, others don't connect their employment with their crime. Some of these offenders are also transient, unemployed or recently released gaol inmates. Basically there are no hard and fast rules relating to work environment or personality type that can pinpoint these types of psychopaths.

Daryl Francis Suckling was an odd jobs man, travelling to various interstate properties and living in caretakers' accommodation or in communal housing. People who knew him described him as a harmless old man who enjoyed his own company, 'wouldn't hurt a fly'. Suckling was also a rapist and a sexual murderer. Both a forensic psychologist and a forensic psychiatrist diagnosed him as having 'antisocial personality disorder'.

The first time he was diagnosed with psychopathy was in 1961 in a Queensland gaol. He would reside at various places throughout NSW, Queensland and Victoria, and do odd jobs in exchange for accommodation. He would frequently go to Melbourne and pick up female prostitutes, one of whom he murdered. Suckling later told a police informant that after killing her, he buried the body but later decided to take further precautions to prevent it from being found, or if found, identified. He told the informer: 'I cut her hands off first and placed them on the bumper bar of the vehicle ... I got the head off next and I put her, put that on the bumper bar.'

Before burying the victim's body the first time, Suckling had already cut off her nipples and vagina to keep as souvenirs. When asked why, Suckling replied: 'I dried them with salt ... and I thought well I'll tan them. I was going to make a tobacco pouch.' He kept these grisly souvenirs in another pouch, which had been seized by the police.

In planning an additional sexual murder, Suckling was also heard to say: 'We're going to have fun with ****. Fuck, this is why I don't want her unconscious, Rohyed out [under the sedative effects of Rohypnol, a date rape drug]. When we start on her she's gotta be half awake, and she'll do what she's fuckin' told because she's in fear of her life.' Suckling was over sixty years old at the time he committed the sexual homicide. It is not known how many others he may have committed and not been caught for.

Seven years after he had performed the sexual homicide, Suckling was making enquiries about moving in with a ninety-four-year-old woman as her full-time carer. He asked people about her medicines, where she kept her bankbooks, etc. None of these people suspected he was a sexual murderer. Suckling was also heard to start organising a government allowance for himself for caring for the elderly or disabled. He was convicted of murder and sentenced 'never to be released' given the heinous nature of his crime.

Murder can be classified as either a stranger homicide, or one in which the offender is known to the victim. In approximately 80 per cent of cases the victim will know their killer. The remaining cases of stranger homicide are usually performed by psychopaths, who have come in contact with the victim either through work or as part of their everyday lives. Other victims are killed as a secondary factor to another crime being committed, for example, a service station attendant killed during an armed robbery.

Sexual assault is another crime where the victim usually knows the offender. In 60 to 80 per cent of sexual assault cases (that are reported to police) the perpetrator is known to the victim. This can include family members, co-workers, tradesmen, masseurs, security guards, 'friends' or a friend of a friend, a husband or wife, clairvoyants, etc. Sexual assault is usually motivated by power, anger and sexuality. Sexuality is the least important of the three motivators, often being used as a weapon to express the power and/or anger.

Stalking is motivated by mental illness, psychopathy, or anger/revenge. It is not uncommon for a stalker to encounter their victim at work. Arsonists are also motivated by a number of factors. Offenders can be psychopaths, mentally ill, or people who are impulsive but not necessarily diagnosable as psychopaths. Motivations include excitement, crime concealment, fraud, pyromania (fascination with setting fires), curiosity, and revenge.

Paedophiles are generally divided into two types; fixated and regressed. Both types of paedophile can encounter their victims where they work. One example would be a paedophile who works in a school as a teacher for easy access to potential victims.

In general, the violent criminal psychopath displays little or no remorse for their behaviours. They regret being caught for their crimes, but do not show significant concern for their victims. They are adept at manipulating systems and people, and quite often convince parole boards to give them another chance as they have seen the error of their ways.

The occupational psychopath

The occupational psychopath is an individual who uses their occupation to satisfy their psychopathic needs while avoiding or minimising punishment. For example, an army officer who fits the profile for a psychopath may use their profession to intimidate and bully subordinates. Giving people orders is a part of an army officer's job, going one step further is not, but can be hidden by the psychopathic officer as part of their duties. They differ from the organisational psychopath in that they do not necessarily want to climb the company ranks, they are happy to feel powerful as a part of their job (even if they go beyond the job requirements to do this). They also differ from the violent criminal psychopath because they do not necessarily inflict physical violence to satisfy their needs, quite often they will use the regulations and systems built into their jobs to control other people. They are not corporate criminal psychopaths because their primary motivation is not the thrill of cheating others or their employer out of money.

Characteristics of the occupational psychopath do overlap significantly with characteristics such as lack of remorse and shallow emotion that are typical of the other sub-types of psychopath. However, they are unique because they are able to use their job to enact their psychopathic tendencies on people and this is not done solely to physically destroy or for financial gain. The people occupational psychopaths come into contact with through their work can be controlled and dominated by bending the rules or using their job to cover their behaviours.

Maurice was working as a uniformed security guard at a large supermarket chain. He had been doing this for three years, and his duties involved preventing shop-lifting and controlling undesirable people in the store. As a licensed security guard, Maurice was legally allowed to carry a baton and handcuffs. By all accounts, he was full of his own self-importance, constantly looked for excitement, lacked responsibility, found it highly amusing that he could steal goods from the store at the same time as 'arresting' other people for the same thing, was impulsive and lost his temper frequently with co-workers, and had no real long-term plans for life.

Maurice used to play mind games with the children he found shoplifting or what he called 'acting suspicious' in the store. A number of children had been dragged out of the store and handcuffed, at which point Maurice threatened to hit them with his baton, and would swing it extremely close to their faces and genital areas. One night Maurice severely assaulted a shoplifter, who was taken to hospital and suffered permanent injuries. When police investigated, it turned out that Maurice had a criminal history,

including assault, car theft, stealing, malicious damage
and domestic violence.

Occupational psychopaths will sometimes set up a
structure or system over a longer period of time to
ensure that their psychopathic needs will be met.
For example, there are a number of what are called
'psychotherapy cults' established where a psychologist
or psychiatrist uses their knowledge of human
behaviour to form a 'cult' and achieve all sorts of
rewards, ranging from money to unlimited access to
sex partners, complete group obedience, or absolute
control over other people's thoughts. Some occupational psychopaths have perverted the occupation
of psychology or psychiatry, using their abilities to
predict and control human behaviour not for the
benefit of their patients, but for their own benefit.

The occupational psychopath's personality characteristics vary. They commonly display no remorse or
feelings of guilt, have manipulative and insincere
behaviours, arrogance, bullying behaviours, parasitic
lifestyles, a grandiose sense of their own self-importance
(often reflected in their occupation), being unreliable
and having shallow emotions that fluctuate frequently.
They can also be impulsive and erratic in terms of
behaviour, not thinking too deeply about the consequences of their actions in the long term.

Because the occupational psychopath displays such
variation in behaviour, not all occupational psychopaths will display every characteristic. For example, the
psychotherapy or other cult leaders usually display

long-term planning (recruiting new members to ensure the cult survives long term) whereas the case study of Maurice, the security guard, showed very little, if any, concern for his long-term future.

Occupational psychopaths can be recognised by their need for power and control over other people, which are acquired at any expense. Like all other psychopaths, they do not have a conscience and feel no remorse or guilt. Everything they do is in their own self-interest.

Why are there different types of psychopath?

As a result of diverse developmental experiences and environmental factors, psychopaths develop different techniques and behaviours to satisfy their need for power, control and domination over other people.

The corporate criminal psychopath, for example, may have been prevented from physically hurting other people, but he or she always got away with stealing money from their parents. Therefore this type of psychopath may have learned that to have money (and the benefits that go along with having money), the easiest way for them to get it is to steal from someone close to them. When they start working, they turn to other methods of getting what they want, and they steal from the company they are working for, as well as their clients and people around them. They get satisfaction out of duping other people, and therefore they do not need to physically hurt and dominate other people.

On the other hand, the violent criminal psychopath may have found higher levels of gratification from being physically violent toward other people rather than simply taking their money or psychologically humiliating them. This childhood pattern is carried on later in life. While the violent criminal psychopath may also steal money (break and enters, car theft, and so on), their true gratification comes from physically hurting people. They often associate physical abuse with psychological control.

The occupational psychopath may have learned as a child that the best way to continue to feel power and control over others is to hide their 'bad behaviour'. They continue to hide their psychopathic behaviours beneath the veneer of their profession, to ensure that they do not experience any interruptions when dominating other people. Or they may simply be taught a set of skills as part of their professional training that makes it easier for them to exploit people legally.

The organisational psychopath may have enjoyed the challenge of psychologically destroying other people when they were young. They may have realised that people naturally followed them, so that when they become adults they continue to play people off against each other in the workplace to ensure they reach the top of the corporate ladder. The financial rewards associated with this rise allow them to buy things and dominating people makes them feel powerful, and the cycle repeats itself as they move between jobs.

Treading on common ground
The different sub-types of psychopath do share some individual and emotional characteristics that make

up their personality. These characteristics are shared because they are fundamental characteristics that guide psychopaths' behaviour and attitude toward life. The characteristics are very similar to those outlined in the Psychopathy Checklist (Revised) as well as Cleckley's Psychopathy Checklist. They are generally accepted by researchers worldwide as being the cornerstones of psychopathy.

Even though psychopaths share common characteristics, differences in behaviour split them into sub-types. These sub-types operate in different ways and are attracted to different work environments.

It should also be noted that psychopaths do not 'switch off' their personalities when they come home to their families, or go out with friends. This means that people who know the psychopath will usually recognise some of the characteristics. If you believe you have a psychopath affecting your life in some way, it is important not to diagnose such a condition yourself. This is because there may be other explanations or diagnoses more appropriate to describe the person's behaviour. Instead, you should contact an appropriately trained professional with experience in dealing with such cases.

Of the people who contact me saying they are 'living with' or 'working with' a psychopath, the majority have incorrectly concluded that the person they are talking about has psychopathy. This does not mean that the people who have contacted me are not suffering or unhappy, it simply means a different course of action must be taken to manage their situation.

4

THE ORGANISATIONAL PSYCHOPATH

JOANNE WAS A thirty-eight-year-old senior accounts manager for a large manufacturing company. She had been in the position for about two years when I was asked to do an assessment of her performance, because most of the staff in her section had either resigned or refused to work with her. As a result of this her section was performing poorly, which impacted on the company's bottom line.

Joanne came across as an articulate, intelligent woman who gave the impression that she was a high achiever in a world that was stacked against her. She explained how difficult it was to perform successfully when other people in the company disliked her, constantly rejected her ideas and insisted that her performance was well below the high standard expected of her. She commented that in her previous jobs she was an excellent people person, was regularly able to sell a large range of products and, in some cases, increase profits by up to 400 per cent. Joanne showed me a reference provided by her previous manager that confirmed all of this.

Looking into Joanne's past, there was nothing outstanding about her in her high school or university years. During her working career she moved from job to job. According to Joanne, she was an exceptional student and was destined for a big career in business or politics. In her mind she believed she was a high achiever. With her good communication skills Joanne was able to talk her way into senior positions.

The organisational psychopath is often regarded by those who first meet him or her as sincere, bright, a good communicator, and powerful. Some co-workers' opinions never change. The organisational psychopath never lets them see beneath the mask he or she presents to the world. Other co-workers are filled with fear and anger at the thought of the same psychopath. Organisational psychopaths use a series of tactics and complicated strategies to manage these discrepant views, facilitating their entry and subsequent rise in the company that unknowingly employed them. A related set of schemes are put in place by the psychopath to circumvent organisational restrictions that may limit their behaviour and subsequent gratification.

Generally when I conduct an assessment for a corporation, I measure both the 'problem' employee's perception of themselves as well as the impressions of those who work for, with and above the employee in question. This process is commonly known as a

360 degree review. However, the questions I ask are very different to most 360 degree reviews, because I am looking for evidence of a specific personality disorder rather than simple dysfunctional behaviour. These questions revolve around the three areas I discussed in the previous chapter as fundamental to identifying an organisational psychopath: organisational/managerial behaviour, interpersonal behaviour and individual/emotional characteristics.

For virtually all questions Joanne rated herself highly favourable. Conversely, her peers, managers and team members generally rated her very poor to extremely poor for the majority of questions. For example, on one question that asked 'Please rate on a scale from −10 to +10 how effective Joanne is at balancing the needs of her team members with her own needs?' (a score of +10 is the most favourable score, while −10 is the least favourable score), Joanne rated herself as +9. Joanne's team members rated her as −8, her peers (other managers at her level) rated her as −4, and Joanne's manager rated her as +2. Interestingly, the senior manager responsible for hiring Joanne rated her as +7 on this characteristic (even though he did not see her interact with her team on a daily basis). A similar pattern was seen for most performance review items.

Joanne's organisational and managerial behaviours were typical of the organisational psychopath. She was rated as highly unethical in terms of business practices, lying whenever the need arose to make herself look good, changing production and sales figures in her favour, and taking credit for the hard work other people had done. She was highly manipulative at an organisational level, spreading rumours about people who she saw as obstacles, berating junior staff, falsifying company documents, claiming for expenses she had not incurred, and generally trying her best to make sure she was always on top in any situation.

She was also universally described as intolerant and arrogant. She saw herself as more intelligent than everyone else in the company. She believed she should have played a more important and senior role in company decisions, and resented the fact that she did not have more power. She also believed that she was doing her staff a favour by putting up with what she believed was their stupidity. She did not take criticism or professional advice well at all. She was completely unpredictable. In one business meeting she simply told the executive team that they had lost her confidence, and walked out.

Joanne was a bully in the workplace. She would threaten people with various things if they did not do exactly as she wanted. Loss of overtime, poor performance reviews and late night shifts for employees with families were just some of the punishments she devised for those she did not like. Her enemies were usually staff members who questioned her authority.

Joanne could not have existed in the company if she did not feed off other people's efforts. For example, she nominated her team for a difficult project, then she went on a 'business trip' while the team was supervised by a relieving manager. When she returned, the team had completed the project, largely due to the guidance of the relieving manager. Joanne immediately began to criticise the relieving manager to her superiors, saying that she had to do all the work when she returned. The person who relieved in her position was never given another chance at managing staff, and eventually resigned. Joanne's motivation for accepting the project, and then taking credit for the relief managers' work, was to be given more power and control in the company by being promoted.

Joanne's interpersonal conduct was as dysfunctional as her organisational and managerial conduct. She was just as manipulative on an interpersonal level as she was at company level. Joanne would continually invent rumours about people, for example, she would tell two people conflicting things, she would offer to help an employee and then officially reprimand them for not doing their duties properly. Joanne was deceitful. All of her team members eventually learned not to believe a word that she said. Some lies were to gain an advantage, such as saying she attended a funeral for time off work, but other lies seemed to serve no purpose.

She was also devious or cunning when it came to coming up with plans to make other people suffer. When she first arrived at the company, she became friends with her manager and the Human Resources manager (before they saw the real Joanne), and convinced them to transfer an older employee who was about to retire into an area he had never worked in before. The retiring employee could not cope with the stress of his new position, and retired before being eligible for certain benefits. He had worked in the company for almost thirty years. Other company employees found Joanne intimidating. Staff felt nervous before speaking with her, particularly as they never knew what would happen and feared being targeted by her.

Joanne was certainly clever enough to manipulate the corporate and legal systems within the company, but did not manage other people's impressions of her well enough to remain in her powerful position. Instead of staying with the one company for long periods of time, she frequently moved between companies, falsifying her résumé and lying her way into more and more senior positions.

Organisational psychopath characteristics
Manipulative organisational behaviour

The organisational psychopath manipulates established social systems in the organisation to cause confusion, furthering their own career or destroying other people's. The organisational psychopath will use deception in his or her manipulation of corporate systems and procedures to minimise their risk of being identified as 'manipulators'. They will also recruit unknowing and unwilling members of the company to help out with their manipulation of corporate politics. The organisational psychopath may also manipulate select company personnel to create a situation advantageous to themselves.

James was a car salesman with ambition. He believed that he was ready for management (after working in the car yard for six months) and was prepared to do whatever it took to get there. James engineered a situation where his fellow workers began to feel used by the management staff, and sales fell as the discontent grew. James continually stirred up the workers' dissatisfaction, constantly creating rumours about management business trips and spending sprees while the salespeople's own base salaries had not changed due to the 'financial downturn'.

At the same time James was liaising with management and undermining his co-workers. Management began to trust James because his advice about the colleagues he was spying on proved to be accurate. James was eventually made team leader in charge of his colleagues, he made work conditions so unpleasant for some of his former 'friends' that they decided to leave. James took control over his workmates and sales rose again, making James look good in the eyes of management. His workmates felt betrayed but could do nothing as management were already suspicious of them and trusted James implicitly.

Unethical behaviour

Accepted moral and professional codes of conduct mean nothing to the organisational psychopath. They will promise more than they are able to deliver, blackmail people to get contracts and to look good in their own company, have sexual relationships with people they have authority or influence over, put in false company records to show work completed that they have not done, and take credit for other people's work. Loopholes in the law are exploited to the full. Generally they see the world as an opportunity, and they will take what they want regardless of the expense to other people. If rules or codes of conduct need to be broken in order to achieve their aims, so be it.

Intolerant/easily bored

The organisational psychopath becomes bored with and intolerant toward situations and people very quickly. They also display very low patience for dealing with the everyday problems and issues facing their staff or fellow workers. In fact, they often see fellow staff as beneath them, and not worth wasting time on unless it provides the organisational psychopath with some pleasure or career benefit. They like to create excitement and stimulation for themselves, whether that be through engineering a crisis or taking a risk with company funds. They may move frequently between jobs as their work routine becomes monotonous, or they may take on a number of roles within the one workplace to ensure constant stimulation. However, taking on a number of jobs or roles in the one company does not mean any one job will be completed. The organisational psychopath rarely finishes anything, they usually 'delegate' to other people or talk their way out of a situation where work has not been produced as promised.

Unpredictable behaviour/shallow emotions

The organisational psychopath is commonly seen as impulsive and erratic in their behaviour. They constantly shift between projects so that their co-workers never know what is happening at any one time. This means that people can never work out what projects the psychopath is working on; whether the job is finished properly. This confusion also allows this type of psychopath to survive, without being discovered, in a constantly changing workplace. The unpredictable nature of the organisational psychopath is closely linked to shallow emotions. The ability to rapidly shift between emotions to correspond with a situation confuses others, allowing the psychopath to deflect attention away from an issue that could reflect negatively on themselves. This sort of behaviour causes fear amongst people who work with the organisational psychopath, as they never know what to expect. This leaves the victims of an organisational psychopath helpless and increases their overall stress levels in the workplace; exactly what the organisational psychopath wants.

Parasitic behaviour

The organisational psychopath is generally a parasite when it comes to surviving, and flourishing in the workplace. Parasitic behaviour includes taking credit for other people's work, conning other people into doing their own work, and/or 'delegating' all of their work to junior staff. There are three main ways the organisational psychopath is able to have other people complete their work for them. First, they may use intimidation and threats to coerce a fellow employee into doing their work. Second, they identify a weak or vulnerable person and deliberately prey on their weak points to manipulate them. Finally, they may present themselves as being helpless or deserving of compassion or sympathy, emotionally blackmailing fellow workers into taking on their duties. Parasitic behaviour is not only confined to the workplace. Often friends and family will be exploited, for example, asking for 'loans' that are never repaid or encouraging parents to mortgage their house so they can indulge themselves.

Undependable and failure to take responsibility for behaviour

Nothing is ever the organisational psychopath's fault, it is always someone else or a breakdown in communication. If a person depends on the organisational psychopath they are highly likely to be let down, at great personal expense to themselves. The psychopath will generously volunteer for projects that will make them look good, and consistently fail to complete their side of the deal. When client contracts are not fulfilled, the organisational psychopath will attempt to avoid responsibility by minimising the consequences, saying such things as 'that is just business' and 'it is survival of the fittest, if they were stupid enough to believe we could fill such an unrealistic contract, they deserve everything they get'.

Being undependable at work can be seen in continual lateness, poor or careless work performance, frequent sick leave and promising to do work that never gets done. Letting people down is usually observed in more than just a work situation, for example, defaulting on loan payments, poor credit history, non-payment of child support, 'forgetting' to pick up the children from school, etc. Responsibility for poor performance or letting co-workers down is denied no matter what evidence exists. The organisational psychopath frequently directs attention away from themselves.

Workplace bullying

Bullying is repeated behaviour that is intended to deliberately make another person feel bad, or cause physical injury. Psychological bullying carried out by the organisational psychopath can include social isolation, humiliation, verbal abuse, unwarranted criticism, intrusive supervision, records being made in personnel files that are unjustified, singling out people for different treatment, physical threats and violence. The organisational psychopath will often go to great lengths to isolate and bully a vulnerable individual, and then create a 'culture of silence'. The 'culture of silence' protects the psychopath because co-workers are too afraid to tell anyone about the suffering they are experiencing. This allows the psychopath to continue their behaviours unchecked.

Seek increased power and control in the company

The organisational psychopath lives for power and control over other people. It makes them feel 'godlike' to know that they hold the fate of other people in their hands and there is nothing that their victims can do about the situation. Having the ability to allocate duties to other staff, to hire and fire staff, to direct the company business strategies in their own favour, to earn more money and be viewed as important, to be allocated private staff to cater to their personal needs all feed this sense of power and control. They do not care so much about other people's opinions of them, and they are not necessarily proud of their increased influence within the company. It is the sense of 'owning' other people that is important for them, along with the challenge of gaining even more power and control in their workplace. The organisational psychopath constantly engages in manipulative strategies and devious, unethical conduct to continue their rise through the organisation's ranks. This climb to the top stimulates the organisational psychopath – it is their 'thrill of the hunt'. This thrill is similar to the thrill felt by the violent criminal psychopath when they are anticipating the crime they will commit.

Create conflict between organisation members

If the organisational psychopath can create conflict between co-workers, it allows them to control their co-workers more easily. The psychopath also finds it satisfying to see people insulting and hurting each other. Generally, conflict is created using two simple strategies.

The first is to select a co-worker who is different from everyone else. This difference may be a physical feature or a personality characteristic (extreme introverts are a favoured target as they are least likely to provide any resistance). The psychopath then manipulates his or her co-workers to ostracise the 'different' person. The victim obviously resists this treatment and there is conflict between the outsider and others in the work group. Depending on how strong the victim is, the conflict can last for a long period of time. This satisfies the psychopath as the attention on them is conveniently deflected. Some organisational psychopaths become 'leaders' by continually instigating the harassment and developing allies in the workplace. These allies can be useful or used to create more conflict. They also provide a power base that support the psychopath in his or her efforts to be promoted.

The second strategy used to create conflict is by spreading rumours about other employees. Using the false rumours the organisational psychopath will create the impression that they have inside information. Managers who are organisational psychopaths will often use rumours to encourage intense competition between team members. This works to safeguard their own position by directing attention toward positions junior to their own.

Louise was a real estate agent working in a suburban office. She was a junior salesperson, and wanted a bigger role in the company as she resented people earning more money than she did when she 'knew' that they could never be as good as she was. Louise was very attractive, and flirted with the salesmen in the office. Louise also invented rumours about another sales-woman, Natalie, who had worked in the office for years. She hoped to make life so unpleasant for Natalie that she would leave and Louise would get her job and salary. Louise pretended to be friends with Natalie, and told her that she should complain about Greg, another salesman in the office, stealing her clients. Very soon, Greg and Louise disliked each other, dragging the rest of the office into their conflict as well. Louise simply watched and manipulated each side to make sure the conflict continued. A once happy office was now extremely dysfunctional.

Interpersonal behaviour
Deceitful/devious/frequent lying

Being deceitful and creating devious strategies in the workplace are a fundamental part of the organisational psychopath's interpersonal conduct. They can quickly work out what people want to hear, and create a story that corresponds with their listener's expectations. Their story is not necessarily well thought out, but the success of the deceit is often dependent on the organisational psychopath's superficial charm and ability to influence a group of people without the group realising what is really happening. Listeners are generally deceived by how the story is told rather than the story's content.

Intimidating behaviour

The organisational psychopath is usually able to identify how far they need to go in order to stand-over and intimidate their co-workers. Psychological vulnerabilities are quickly identified and ruthlessly exploited. For example, a person who lacks self-confidence may be the subject of verbal ridicule by the psychopath in front of their co-workers because they dared to criticise or stand up to the psychopath. The organisational psychopath is not above making physical threats either. People who have experienced such a psychopath in the workplace have recounted that something about the psychopath was menacing, making them feel scared, as though the psychopath had far greater power and influence, and they did not dare to cross or upset them. This threat of intimidation is enhanced by co-workers seeing what happens to those who stand up to the psychopath. Victims eventually leave, are transferred to another section, become extremely miserable or are continually bullied by the psychopath. The one thing that co-workers find most alarming is the emotional detachment of the psychopath – their cold indifference and doing whatever is necessary to achieve their goal is truly frightening.

Charming/superficial

The organisational psychopath can be very charming, taking control of a conversation or group of people and leading them in any direction that serves the psychopath's needs. They will tell witty stories, know how to make people laugh (often at someone else's expense), and are generally very entertaining. Often the organisational psychopath appears to be knowledgeable in a wide range of areas. When caught out by a more informed listener, they are unfazed and will change the topic or encourage their critic to expand on their subject area so the psychopath will not be caught out the next time. The psychopath might bully their way through conversation, and by sheer force of their charm and personality, people will believe them. If questioned about their facts the organisational psychopath will attempt to steer the conversation in another direction. When the organisational psychopath's lack of knowledge is found out, they show very little if any concern, and gloss over the gap in their story by reworking the facts. Some organisational psychopaths are very proud of their ability to persuade people to do things they would not normally do by using their charm and good communication skills.

Tactics and strategies of the organisational psychopath

A number of issues are important when looking at the organisational psychopath's corporate survival and career development. These issues can be addressed by answering specific questions, including how does the psychopath select a particular place of employment? What tactics do they use to enter the organisation they have selected? How do they pass the 'stringent' recruitment process that is supposed to identify the best employee? How do they interact with their co-workers, and what relationship does this interaction have with how they are promoted in the company? Why are they not detected as a psychopath in the company when they are causing such misery and suffering for the people around them? How do they hide amongst the other employees? How do they do their work when they are prone to boredom, impulsiveness, parasitic behaviour, etc? Is there a strategy they use to escape being held accountable for poor performance? How do they manipulate other people into doing their work for them?

Answering each of these questions significantly reduces the chance of a psychopath being employed by and creating confusion in a workplace. The organisational psychopath can be detected and an intervention put in place at any of the stages described below. Obviously the earlier they are detected the less damage they can do to the company and/or the people around them.

Corporate recruitment – organisational psychopath wanted

We know that the organisational psychopath, like other psychopaths, is often prone to boredom, easily frustrated, constantly looking for new and exciting things, and enjoys having power over other people. They are also prepared to do whatever it takes to achieve their aims, regardless of the cost to others. Management is a broad job category that provides the opportunity for the psychopath to take charge over other people, not necessarily be involved in the details of a job, and constantly move from one project to the next. The organisational psychopath also feels entitled to large monetary rewards given their narcissistic and egocentric nature. Management positions often pay well.

Consider the following job advertisements:

'You will be innovative with something special to offer. No doubt you will have leadership and influencing skills, and be able to WOW a sceptical selection panel. We want someone who can see the biggest picture and have broad impact. Your background could be in...whatever, you will be someone special.' Salary $150K+.

This position was a senior management position (national loss prevention manager) in which the successful applicant could also quite easily steal on a large scale from the company.

'Advertising manager wanted...you will need to have professional communication skills and be motivated to meet deadlines regardless.' Salary $80K+.

'Area manager wanted for young, entrepreneurial company with big ambitions. Huge career opportunity for outstanding talent, make a real difference and accelerate your career. Get out of corporate bureaucracy and put your career on a fast track. The person we are looking for will be an entrepreneur at heart and want to shape the business, be a high achiever, thrive on achieving great results, and be prepared to challenge conventions.' Salary negotiable.

'You will have a strong desire to achieve, the capacity to persuade and influence others,

excellent communication skills... You want to work with the best. You enjoy competing as much as winning. You believe in high rewards for high levels of performance.' Salary $85K.

The last advertisement attracted an organisational psychopath who was ultimately recruited. If I were doing a study in which I needed to find organisational psychopaths, I would place advertisements similar to those above in the employment section of newspapers. In fact, some researchers in America did just that. They advertised for 'adventurous people who have led exciting lives... charming people who are irresponsible but good at handling people'. They had a number of sub-criminal psychopaths reply to their advertisements.

It is clear from the advertisements above that glib and superficial charm, lack of remorse or guilt (motivated to meet deadlines regardless), proneness to boredom (get out of the corporate bureaucracy, challenge conventions) are all characteristics that some corporations are advertising for. Obviously these corporations are not looking for a psychopath, however the advertisements they have placed may well appeal to the organisational psychopath, as well as non-psychopaths.

American organisational psychologist Dr Paul Babiak also reports that the organisational psychopath finds organisations that are in a constant state of transition and organisational change more desirable. This is because the organisational psychopath is able to use the confusion within the company to hide their behaviours. Also, the organisational psychopath enjoys the unstructured work environment of a corporation that is changing. They can get away with their idiosyncratic behaviours more easily because they are seen as 'creative' and 'dynamic', just what the company needs to move forward in a difficult business world.

The job application and interview – entering the organisation

Contrary to what people imagine, the organisational psychopath finds it particularly easy to win positions in a wide range of companies. One organisational psychopath I was asked to assess told me that he deserved a much higher salary. He threatened to leave and get a new job as a manager, boasting that he could do this within one month. He left and was working in a more senior position for a rival firm within two weeks.

When it comes to recruitment, most companies either use a recruitment firm or hire employees directly. Employee selection is largely based on the quality of the applicants' résumés, verbal skills and impression management in the job interview, and sometimes referee checks. Performance in previous jobs is also analysed in some positions, however 'performance' usually refers to how much money/ sales/accounts, etc, the applicant was responsible for. Again, this information is often disclosed directly by the job applicant and is therefore able to be falsified as the previous employer is hardly likely to disclose such sensitive business information. That, of course, is presuming they know their employee has applied for another job at all.

In the corporate world, the résumé is the most effective tool for identifying people with a specific skill set desired by an organisation. It is not a good tool for detecting whether an applicant is an organisational psychopath, or indeed any type of psychopath. Generally people who read CVs are not trained to detect deception, they simply check a list of desirable attributes, rank the applications, and then notify applicants they have an interview. There are specialist firms one can hire to check the truthfulness of a résumé. In my experience, these firms are not trained to detect psychopathy, and therefore are ineffective when it comes to preventing such a person from gaining employment in a company. Moreover, these firms often take referee's reports at face value, failing to check a referee's relationship with the applicant. Organisational psychopaths I have asked state that it is just as easy to get a job when applying directly to the company or going through a recruitment firm. What is important for them is identifying what the company/recruiter wants to read in the application, and giving it to them.

After the résumé screening process comes the interview phase. The organisational psychopath excels at this stage of the recruitment process. They use their charm and excellent verbal skills with tremendous effect, presenting a picture of the perfect candidate for the position.

Corporate reconnaissance

Once the organisational psychopath enters an organisation, they evaluate the people they will be working
with, as well as the corporate systems that shape their
working conditions. This is true of any new employee,
psychopath and non-psychopath, it is natural to
evaluate your new surroundings and co-workers. The
organisational psychopath immediately tries to identify
the usefulness of particular colleagues and loopholes in
the corporate systems that will allow them to do what
they want without interruption by the people who
enforce company rules. The organisational psychopath
also identifies weakness and vulnerability displayed by
various colleagues that can be exploited if need be at a
later date.

The organisational psychopath works out who will
be useful and then creates an impression that will
appeal to that particular person. It is not uncommon
for senior management, human resources managers,
supervisors and co-workers to have different impressions of the same organisational psychopath. This is
because the organisational psychopath has identified
how useful each of these people can be, and for the
'chosen few' seen as useful, a specific impression is
created.

The level of power and influence a person has in the
organisation is the most important evaluation criteria
used by the psychopath. Senior managers, who
often have very little to do with the organisational
psychopath on a day-to-day basis, are charmed by this
type of psychopath, and see them as a promising

employee who needs to be looked after. The organisational psychopath will generally choose a specific target amongst senior management, doing similar activities (jogging, drinking after work, children at the same school, shopping, finishing and starting work at the same time) to allow frequent contact and eventual 'friendship'.

They will also try to charm the senior manager's personal assistant, giving them access to the senior manager at any time. The personal assistant also validates the senior manager's opinion of the organisational psychopath if ever he or she is asked. When this strategy is successful, the organisational psychopath has cleverly cultivated a very powerful ally in the organisation, who often tells the other senior managers about this 'promising employee'. Senior managers are usually intelligent people, who cannot afford to be wrong, particularly in front of their colleagues. Once their mind is made up it is difficult to change as senior managers are hesitant in recognising they have made a mistake about a person they thought they knew. It is only after repeated incidents are brought to their attention that they are forced to agree there 'may' be a problem, and establish a system to look into it.

Colleagues at the same level as the organisational psychopath are generally treated well while the psychopath settles in. They often report that the person was charming, fun to be with, made them feel good, intelligent, and was always there when needed. The psychopath appears to be everyone's friend, but in reality they are setting up their colleagues as 'unfavourable employees' to eliminate the competition when promotion time comes around. The first the victim knows of this 'back-stabbing' campaign is when they either complain about the psychopath (and are told the psychopath has already put in numerous complaints about them), or when they do not get the promotion they deserve. It is at this point that the psychopath's colleagues realise the true nature of their 'friend', but it is too late to do anything as he or she is usually senior to them and their complaints are often seen as malicious.

Colleagues junior to the psychopath are treated in a similar way. Generally they are conned into thinking the psychopath is their ally, until they become aware they have been used to further the psychopath's career, or simply for the psychopath's entertainment. These employees belong to one of the following three groups.

The first group are the employees who follow the psychopath. Initially they follow because the organisational psychopath makes them feel good about themselves, part of a group, and always have fun around them. Later, they follow out of fear; fear of being excluded from the group or even fear of being the group's next victim.

The second group, junior employees, are the vulnerable ones, the targets for bullying and harassment. The bullying and harassment campaign usually establishes the psychopath as leader of the group, as well as keeping him or her amused. However, some organisational psychopaths encourage and manipulate the group from behind the scenes, spreading rumours in one-on-one as opposed to group situations. They appear to be friends with everyone when really they are controlling the entire situation.

The third group are those who are kept on side for the time the psychopath is with the organisation. These employees are used by the psychopath to complete their work, make them look good and keep them out of trouble. The organisational psychopath plays on vulnerabilities of people within this group, such as insecurity about looks, weight, intelligence, a need to feel wanted, and so on. They are not beneath having sex with junior employees who feel unattractive, or they tell those who feel unintelligent that they can prove how smart they are by doing whatever the psychopath tells them to do. Organisational psychopaths use people's weaknesses and tell them what they want to hear in return for work being completed. Some employees are bullied into doing the psychopath's work for them. They are threatened with dismissal, or they learn that to avoid being harassed by the psychopath all they need to do is some extra work on behalf of the psychopath. These victims may resist for a while, but often learn that the easiest way is to do the psychopath's work or leave the company.

Dr Paul Babiak reports similar findings in American corporations who have experienced the organisational psychopath. In what Babiak calls the 'assessment' phase, the psychopath 'quickly assesses the utility of organisation members and can quickly charm them into being supporters. Co-workers' utility (to the psychopath) is based on position, power, technical abilities, access to information, and control of resources' (Babiak, 1995, p. 16). In other words, the organisational psychopath values powerful people, people able to do their work for them, people with access to information the psychopath needs, and people who control the corporate systems such as building access and auditors.

Often organisational psychopaths will try to be friends with those who control company resources, such as security personnel and holders of the company records. However, these people, such as auditors, human resources and quality control personnel, whose role it is to check on employees are the natural enemy of the psychopath and very quickly detect the underlying nature of such individuals. These employees are not easily manipulated or conned, as they rely on hard cold figures to analyse what is going on rather than the psychopaths' verbal promises of what will happen in the future. When these people try to raise any concerns they are not listened to by those in authority because the organisational psychopath has already set up the foundations to protect their position.

Organisational manipulation

Once the organisational psychopath has established how the company works, and how useful each colleague is, they set in motion a series of strategies that help them rise through the company ranks. As they are promoted higher in the company, the organisational psychopath has greater power and control over the people around them. Often it is when they reach the higher levels in an organisation that they implement strategies designed to cause unnecessary stress for their workers, for no other reason than to watch them suffer.

The number and type of strategies used by the organisational psychopath to move their way up through the ranks varies. This is because the organisational psychopath is an intelligent, charming manipulator who reacts to each situation differently. The general aims of manipulative strategies implemented in the early stages of the organisational psychopath's career are threefold.

Using their particular manipulative/organisational behaviours outlined on p. 59 the organisational psychopath aims to:

- create disharmony between co-workers;
- spread disinformation;
- portray themselves in the best possible light.

The first aim is to create disharmony between co-workers. In this confusion, the psychopath is able to play people against one another without them realising what is happening. Simultaneously, the organisational psychopath is able to endear themselves to management by resolving seemingly intractable situations. They demonstrate their leadership ability at the expense of their supervisor, who does not appear to be capable of resolving the situation created by the psychopath.

The second aim is to spread disinformation about rivals within the company. These rivals include co-workers at the same level as the psychopath as well as people in positions senior to the psychopath. Generally this disinformation is spread through the use of third parties within the organisation. For example, the organisational psychopath may befriend a secretary or delivery person who has frequent contact with everyone in the organisation. The psychopath then tells this person a rumour, or series of rumours about a specific target, knowing that these rumours will rapidly spread around the organisation. They may also sabotage other people's work, palm off unachievable tasks to co-workers so that failure is inevitable, conceal problems from a supervisor until the last minute so the supervisor does not produce what is expected of them, and criticise a boss to senior management directly, ignoring the chain of command.

The third aim of the psychopaths' manipulative strategies is impression management – to portray themselves in the best light possible. This is achieved by taking credit for other people's work (or even stealing it), creating crises and then 'saving the day' in a very noticeable way, exaggerating their achievements, bypassing the chain of command to impress senior managers directly, having third parties spread positive rumours about them, volunteering for extra projects and never completing them, searching for projects that will get them high exposure within the company, and cutting costs and overworking employees in the short term to secure a promotion without considering the fallout for the company.

Once the organisational psychopath is in a managerial or supervisory position, they use a number of tactics to cause confusion and stress amongst employees. Some of the more common techniques include restrictive or intrusive supervision, where employees are given very little or no autonomy in how they do their work. This creates a feeling of loss of ownership and causes tension and frustration. The work done by employees will either not be recognised, be described as inadequate, or credit for the work will be taken by the psychopath. This discourages new ideas, decreases productivity, and perpetuates mediocre performance, which are then noted on employee files in case an employee becomes a threat to the organisational psychopath.

Employees may also be given monotonous jobs to do, effectively removing any interest in coming to work. Again this de-motivating factor causes high levels of stress for the targeted person. After a while, employees become extremely frustrated, sometimes reacting aggressively. All of these behaviours are diligently recorded on their personnel files by the organisational psychopath. Employees are given little or no opportunity to develop new skills or ideas, they are not given any positive feedback about their work, they are pressured into doing unpaid overtime to keep their jobs, and they are not promoted but are asked to do higher level work. The list of 'punishments' is long, limited only by the organisational psychopath's imagination.

To escape responsibility for incomplete or unsatisfactory work, the organisational psychopath blames others. Most commonly, they will blame another section in the company for holding up the process, or a subordinate for not producing the work on time. Usually these excuses are lies. However, no one really detects these lies as the psychopath makes sure never to have all parties involved in the same room at the same time. Therefore it is easy to continue to spread lies about the individual parties as they are never there to defend themselves. Eventually the poor work performance is forgotten, or put in the 'too hard basket' and the psychopath has escaped detection once again. Dr Paul Babiak, an industrial organisational psychologist, found that the psychopaths who were disrupting some of the companies he was consulting for consistently spent more time socialising face-to-face or on the telephone, avoiding group meetings.

The organisational psychopath is also unpleasant to employees on an interpersonal level. They are often sarcastic, aggressive, intimidating, play or encourage extreme practical jokes, condescending, ignore people or give them the 'silent treatment', lose their temper, may sexually harass employees, are never available to talk with employees, ambush employees in front of other supervisors, shout at employees. The abuse can be never-ending.

Discovery and conflict

Dr Paul Babiak has identified three groups that emerge as a result of the psychopath's behaviour within any organisation. The first group of employees are those who initially liked the organisational psychopath, and were charmed into thinking he or she was a friend when in fact they were being exploited. These employees come from all levels of the organisation, and are initially supporters of the psychopath. Once these supporters are no longer useful to the psychopath, they are abandoned.

A second group of employees become aware of the true nature of the psychopath, and see how they and the organisation are being manipulated. This makes them feel frustrated, angry, used and they seek some sort of retribution. They frequently confront the psychopath, or senior management, but are usually brushed off as the psychopath has been complaining about them for a long period of time to his or her 'friend' who is a senior manager. Babiak says that the psychopath uses the people who support them in the organisation to neutralise anyone who complains about their behaviour.

Babiak also points out that these internal conflicts between people cause demoralised staff and lowered production levels, as well as team disintegration. Interestingly, he has found that the executives at the top of the organisation usually have no idea about the true cause of the lowered productivity, they are unaware that an organisational psychopath is causing enormous internal damage to their organisation.

The final thrill for the organisational psychopath is to turn on the higher level/high power individuals (or patrons) in the company who once protected them. The 'psychopath manipulates not only individuals but the whole power structure in his/her favour. The patrons are then the big losers, as they become the patsies' (Babiak, 1995, p. 16). The cycle of betraying people at higher and higher levels of the company continues until either the organisational psychopath is detected and asked to leave, or the organisational psychopath reaches as high a level in the company as is possible for them.

The organisational psychopath uses a combination of strategies to manipulate the workplace situation to their own advantage. They enter an organisation by lying or embellishing information about themselves; intimidate, bully, con and manipulate both their co-workers and the organisation, and are promoted up the company ranks.

Once they are detected as an organisational psychopath, they are either made redundant or offered an attractive package to leave the company. Unfortunately the higher up the promotional ladder they are, the less likely it is they will be identified because they can camouflage their behaviour more easily by silencing critics.

5

THE CORPORATE CRIMINAL PSYCHOPATH

SHARON WAS A local bank manager. She had been with the bank for over twenty-five years, and in that time worked her way up to a position where she was not heavily scrutinised when it came to issuing housing loans. She lived in a middle-class suburban neighbourhood with her husband. The couple had no children; instead they concentrated on work and business. Sharon was involved in many community activities and people around her saw her as a 'normal' member of their community. She seemed to fit in with everybody and was always there to help when asked.

When Sharon was not working at the bank, or at home tending her garden, she was indulging herself with million(s) stolen from her employer. She would come in to work early and stay behind after everyone else had left. It was not uncommon for her to 'pop in' on the weekend to process loan applications that she did not have time to complete during the week. The reality was that Sharon was processing her own loan applications, lending herself money under the guise of numerous aliases she had created. Sharon would falsify a computer loan application for fictitious people, lending 'them' amounts ranging from $285,000 to $430,000. Sharon knew that if her scheme was to work, she would have to pay the interest on each of the false loans, or the bank would foreclose and demand the money back, and they would also discover that a fictitious person had taken out the loan. So Sharon kept enough money to make the payments on each loan. The fraud only came to notice when a bank audit revealed that a number of loans had correspondence going to one address; an apartment in one of the most expensive suburbs in Perth.

Sharon used the money to rent a luxury apartment on the waterfront, where she threw expensive parties and kept all the luxury items she bought. She took first-class holidays overseas and bought a luxury car. When police executed a search warrant on the apartment, they found room after room filled with original paintings, antiques, expensive electrical goods and furniture. Jewellery and cosmetics were also found throughout the luxury apartment.

Sharon is now serving a gaol sentence for her fraudulent behaviours. She helped the bank recover all the property she purchased and pleaded guilty to the frauds. It is not clear whether Sharon pleaded guilty out of remorse or to reduce her gaol time – it is unlikely she would admit to playing the system. Some people around

Sharon still believe that she is 'not a bad person', just someone who took the wrong path. Sharon never expressed any remorse for her behaviour, nor did she voluntarily stop stealing money.

White-collar corporate criminal psychopaths

Jeff was a twenty-four-year-old accountant in a large marketing firm. He was frustrated that the company could not see his potential for doing more important work rather than processing payments. He also believed he was under-paid. He displayed other psychopathic characteristics such as glib and superficial verbal abilities, lack of remorse for his behaviours, was prone to boredom, was sexually promiscuous, irresponsible, displayed parasitic behaviours, pathological lying and a grandiose sense of his own self-worth.

Jeff decided he would teach the company a lesson and make some money for himself at the same time. He set up a 'shelf company'. He then designed an exclusive-looking letterhead for a very general sounding company, and rented a post office box for all correspondence. He wrote a bill to the company he worked for, from his 'shelf company', charging them for services that had never been rendered. One of Jeff's responsibilities was to process incoming bills, writing out the cheques and then giving these cheques to a more senior accountant to sign (an anti-fraud measure). He would process his own bill, write out a cheque and hand it to the senior accountant. The bill was paid without question.

He continued doing this until he was finally caught when a company auditor tried to contact Jeff's 'shelf company' and found that it was false. When the police fraud squad investigated, they discovered that the bank accounts linked to the shelf company belonged to Jeff. For over six months Jeff had fraudulently obtained approximately $100,000. Only $4,000 was recovered from his bank account at the time of his arrest. He had spent the rest on rent for a luxury apartment, holidays to first-class hotels, alcohol, restaurants and parties.

The corporate criminal psychopath generally displays more long-term planning than the violent criminal and occupational psychopath. They often develop their strategy over longer periods of time, testing the security systems to minimise their chances of being caught. They also work very hard at managing people's opinions of them. They want to be viewed as a diligent and honest worker so that they will be seen as a low security risk. Once they have this classification (whether it be formal or informal security classifications) they are often promoted into positions that make it easy for them to steal from the company. This opportunity to commit large-scale frauds often occurs in a position where they are not directly accountable to anyone when it comes to the financial decisions they make on behalf of the company.

There is no common age for the corporate criminal psychopath. Offenders have been caught from their early twenties to their late seventies. They come from all social backgrounds, rich and poor families, and they may or may not have a family of their own. Often they use their fraudulent activity to impress their friends as it allows them to live a lifestyle beyond their own means and what others can afford. Corporate fraud is one type of psychopathy in which female offenders are almost as prevalent as male offenders.

A number of behavioural factors are particular to the corporate criminal psychopath in the workplace. Generally the psychopathy characteristics are not noticed until after the person is caught, as the corporate criminal psychopath manages to conceal their true nature from the casual observer. The following characteristics are not necessarily indicative of corporate criminal psychopathy. People with a combination of the psychopathy characteristics and the behaviours listed are more likely to be involved in white-collar fraud. Behaviours that are easily observable by fellow employees include: working unusually long hours; resisting being promoted out of their current position; refusing to take annual leave; and purchasing things that are obviously above their salary level, such as luxury cars or overseas trips.

Sudden changes in an employee's spending habits or lifestyle, frequent unexplained absences from work, missing or altered company records of financial transactions, excessive billing expenses, a very close relationship between an employee and a client, excessive overtime and the same billing address for different accounts are also indicative factors. The more of these behaviours that are observed, the higher the chance a corporate fraud is being committed. The presence of psychopathy characteristics further increases this risk.

After the fraud has been committed, the corporate criminal psychopath has to conceal their behaviour. Signs of this deception include an employee who frequently ignores internal company policy for accounting systems, a person in charge of sales who has a very close relationship with the accounts staff responsible for their clients, 'creative' book-keeping to ensure everything balances when the auditors check, and ignoring management requests to justify particular financial irregularities as they are 'too busy' to waste time.

The corporate criminal psychopath's strategy can generally be summarised as follows. They enter the company, make connections with the people they later use to cover up their behaviour, and then find a 'weak point' in the corporate system. This allows them to steal large amounts of money and escape detection for long periods of time. It is not uncommon for a corporate criminal psychopath to remain undetected until after a company collapses and the books are thoroughly examined. Alternatively, they are often caught by chance when they go off sick or on holiday and their replacement notices that a fraud has been committed.

The person most likely to fraudulently steal money from a company and get away with it is a long-term, trusted employee who knows the corporate systems used to monitor financial transactions. However, white-collar fraud is not limited to long-term employees. Contract workers, employees who join the company with the specific purpose of stealing money, and employees who have been recruited as 'graduates' are also capable of committing fraud. In fact, any employee is capable. What differs is various employees' ability to escape detection over long periods of time. People outside a company can also commit white-collar fraud, however it has been estimated that 85 per cent of frauds are committed by people inside the company.

Like other types of crime, the offender who commits fraud is not necessarily a psychopath. Dr Russell Smith of the Australian Institute of Criminology has claimed that greed is the offender's primary motivation in almost a third of fraud cases. While greed and supporting a lifestyle a psychopath is not entitled to provides one explanation for committing fraud, gambling and drug addictions are equally prominent motives. In fact, one of the major signs to look for as a corporation is employees who regularly take two and three-hour lunch breaks, as lunch is a prime time for them to indulge in their gambling addictions. While gamblers and drug addicts can be diagnosed as having psychopathy in addition to their addiction, not all of them actually show the characteristics needed to be diagnosed as a psychopath.

Some corporations run fraud awareness training for their employees, with varying degrees of success. The success or failure of the awareness program is directly related to the training program used by the consultant. Generally a good program includes teaching employees to become 'behavioural profilers', recognising how the corporate criminal psychopath conceals their crime. Management and auditors are also taught why it is so important to make detailed examinations of over-time records, sick leave patterns, client accounts, and randomly checking invoices received from external suppliers. One very effective technique is to compare an employee's work with that of a replacement when the employee is sick or on holiday. If there are discrepancies this provides a compelling reason to investigate further.

I also suggest that companies include their human resources department in these fraud reduction training sessions. The easiest way to avoid having money stolen by an employee is not to employ a corporate criminal psychopath in the first place. It is important to check referees reports thoroughly (including who the referee is), as well as checking that the prospective employee is who they claim to be. Some psychopaths get a job using false identification documents with the specific purpose of stealing from the company and then leaving. By the time the fraud is detected, they have disappeared completely.

Often the corporate criminal psychopath has plausible explanations for large lies in their résumé, but when it comes to small details that do not make sense they have no explanation. Therefore it is important to recognise that every last detail must be double checked when an employee is entering a position that gives them access to large amounts of money in a company.

Blue-collar corporate criminal psychopaths

Joe was a service technician for a high-end market electronic goods manufacturer. Whenever people had a problem with their $20,000 products, they were sent to Joe for repair or a destruction order for the goods that were beyond repair. Joe used to mark down a number of items as 'beyond repair'. This would make the customer happy, as they would receive a brand new item. Joe would take the item home and repair the minor problem at little expense to himself. He would then sell the items for $15,000, much cheaper than the recommended price. Every time Joe did this he made $15,000. No one in the company ever checked what happened to the items that were marked as 'beyond repair' until a customer returned a 'destroyed' item he had purchased from Joe.

Not all psychopaths work in white-collar positions that allow them to steal large sums of money. The corporate criminal psychopath often starts in a job that allows them to steal property from their employer. Alternatively, they may not be confident or intelligent enough to con their way into a high-paying job that gives them access to large amounts of money. Similar to white-collar corporate criminals, not all blue-collar criminals are psychopaths. Psychopathy can only be determined by examining whether the cluster of psychopathy characteristics is present.

A number of behavioural indicators can be used to 'profile' a blue-collar corporate criminal psychopath. Perhaps the biggest indicator of theft is a refusal by an employee to be promoted out of their position. Often this is because they are 'earning' significantly more than their salary by stealing items.

The blue-collar psychopath may also park their vehicle closer to the loading dock to steal goods, work very early or late when no one else is around, mark down prices of items they are going to buy, keep money received for goods and not process them at the cash register, have a very close group of friends who are also very secretive (that is, also involved in stealing), pay cash for very expensive items, appear to live beyond their means, have very high rates of no sales, refunds, etc, and have sudden unexplained reductions in sales revenue every now and then. Finally, it is not uncommon for them to ask questions about the operations of corporate areas that do not concern them.

The self-employed corporate criminal psychopath – con artists

Jenny had been a sales assistant at an electrical store for twelve years. She was forty-one years old, and had a thirteen-year-old son from a relationship that lasted fifteen years before Jenny asked her partner to leave after he had one affair too many. Jenny described the subsequent battle for custody of their child as well as maintenance payments as difficult and emotionally draining. Jenny was very stressed, and relied heavily on her family to help her out with financial matters as she was just making enough money to survive. She managed to make her weekly rent payments, purchase groceries and some gifts for her child, and made do with what she already had as she could not afford new things.

One day she was working in the shop when a man came in and started talking to her about what a great store it was and a variety of other topics. He introduced himself as Mike, and asked her if she wanted to go out for dinner and a drink after work. Jenny had never felt appreciated like this before and accepted, organising with her mother to look after her son. She described Mike as polite, respectful and very attentive, a real gentleman.

Mike boasted about himself. He claimed that he was a property developer from Melbourne. He said that he had just sold a house for $2 million and was waiting for the cheque to come through. He and Jenny would go out looking at houses and luxury cars so that when the cheque finally came though they could have a life together. Mike also claimed that he was a former special forces commando, was close friends with a high profile Australian businessman, had mafia connections, and he would not hesitate to do anything to protect Jenny and her son, including killing someone. Jenny believed all of this as it was said so convincingly. Mike brought these things up every now and then. Later Jenny realised that he was setting her up to be afraid of him when she realised that he was a con artist.

Every now and then, Mike would ask Jenny for $50 to cover expenses, or $100 to fix his car. He told Jenny that she could take it out of the money she kept for rent and bills as he would cover them when his cheque came through. Jenny fell behind on her rent as she lent Mike more and more money. Mike also befriended Jenny's son and 'invested' his entire life savings for him. The money was 'invested' and lost in the poker machines at the local RSL club. Mike also took Jenny's money to 'invest' as he assured her that she had no idea when it came to business and that he would fix it for her. She believed his story.

Eventually, when the promised cheque failed to materialise, Mike became more aggressive to Jenny. He called her stupid, and would sometimes hit her, apologising for his behaviour afterwards. He would tell her that he loved her and he could not handle the stress of waiting for their cheque. Jenny wanted to believe him, so she went along with his lies.

One night Jenny was cooking dinner for Mike (he was living in her home until his cheque came through) but he never came home. He simply disappeared out of Jenny and her son's life forever. Jenny's son was devastated, his life savings gone and a man he thought of as a father figure had deceived him. No one knows where Mike is to this day. It turns out that Mike's real name was James, and he was well known as a serial fraud offender to police in most states of Australia. He was an expert at preying on vulnerable women until he was discovered, at which point he moved on to his next victim. Mike was also heavily involved in defrauding companies of money, stealing credit cards and reusing them, and cashing fraudulent cheques.

Individuals like Mike are classified as corporate criminal psychopaths because their fraudulent behaviour is akin to obtaining money by deception used against corporations. Their behaviour is criminal, and ruthless as it exploits weakness and vulnerability that is often beyond the victim's control.

The corporate criminal psychopath who defrauds individuals instead of companies characteristically relies on people's greed and/or low self-esteem as the 'lubricant' that helps them to commit their crimes. As a general rule, they promise their victims very high returns on their investment. The victim is usually told they do not need to do any work at all to make more money, all they have to do is count their money as it multiplies. When the victim becomes suspicious after promised returns do not materialise, the psychopath uses their superior verbal abilities to reassure the victim. The victim often goes along with the psychopath's deception, as they do not want to believe that they have lost their hard earned money. It is also not uncommon for victims to invest additional sums of money with the corporate criminal psychopath even after they become suspicious of the scheme. They invest the additional money because the psychopath is able to convince them that they will make even more money if they just contribute 'a little more'. The con-artist uses a number of stages when coning their victims.

Stage 1: Meeting the target
The corporate criminal psychopath introduces themselves and bombards their victim with so much information that there is no time for their victim to think. Because the victim has no time to evaluate what the psychopath is saying, they are more likely to believe it. The psychopath often throws in compliments that

make the victim feel good about themselves. Therefore the victim, who has often been selected because they are lonely or have low self-esteem, likes being with the psychopath because they feel good about themselves and their lives, something they have usually not experienced in a long time. At this stage, the corporate criminal psychopath is friendly and appears willing to do anything to please their victim.

Stage 2: Establishing rapport

The psychopath remains close to the victim, eliminating their ability to discuss the psychopath's behaviour with other people who are not emotionally involved in the situation. The psychopath maintains this rapport by taking the person out to dinners, looking for houses, picnics and so on. The psychopath is making sure the victim's false perception of them is deeply ingrained.

Stage 3: Identify victim needs

The psychopath cleverly works out what the victim needs to hear so they can successfully con the victim. The psychopath identifies emotional weak points for the victim, such as not feeling loved, greed for more money, insecurity about financial future, desire to provide financial wealth for their family, dreams of owning country property, luxury car, finding happiness, the list goes on. The psychopath then creates a set of lies that suggest or promise this need will be satisfied as long as the victim continues to trust the psychopath. The victim usually has to prove they trust the psychopath by giving them sums of money.

Stage 4: Create emotional pain

When the victim starts questioning and doubting the psychopath's promises, the behaviour changes. Still preying on the victim's emotional weak points, the psychopath now starts to attack them rather than boosting their self-esteem. They may threaten the victim, or imply that a person with already low self-esteem is 'stupid' for not trusting the psychopath, or ask how family members will feel when they realise they have been cheated out of millions of dollars by the victim's lack of trust in the psychopath. They emphasise how the victim will feel if the emotional and physical dreams the psychopath has promised them are not satisfied. Because the victim has imagined their dreams being fulfilled, it is very difficult for them to abandon these dreams. Because the victim wants to believe their dreams will be fulfilled, they contribute additional money. Psychologically it is very difficult for a victim to admit they have been conned.

Stage 5: Reverse psychology

When the victim questions the con-artist about the scheme, the psychopath states that maybe the victim really does not deserve to have their dreams fulfilled, as they do not have the courage or determination to achieve them, even with the psychopath's help. The victim, who trusted, and often still does trust the psychopath, injects even more money into the 'scheme' to prove their commitment to the psychopath. The psychopath often pretends that the additional money injected is not enough to regain their 'trust' in the victim's commitment, the victim is emotionally worse off than when they first met the fraudster. On top of being set up to lose a significant amount of money they are emotionally crushed, not to mention the indignity of knowing they have been conned. The victims have very little confidence in their own ability to make any decisions because the one time they trusted someone with everything proved to be the biggest mistake of their lives.

Consumer and investment scams

Consumer scams are another way a corporate criminal psychopath can deceive a larger number of victims, not to mention the larger amounts of money they can access. The most common consumer scams involve property, superannuation, and investment schemes in which real estate is sold at over-inflated prices, or the victim invests their money with the corporate criminal psychopath only to have the psychopath and their money disappear. Generally these seminar type schemes use the same principles and stages as the personal corporate criminal psychopath. For example, property, superannuation and investment seminars generally open with an introduction where the presenter introduces the victims to dreams of financial independence or something similar. Rapport is then established by introducing 'testimonies' of people with similar backgrounds to the victims. Needs of the audience are pinpointed with questions such as 'Would you like to be a millionaire in five years with just a $10,000 investment?' Generally the needs of the victims are centred around financial success.

The seminar presenter then creates emotional pain by pointing out to the audience that they are not millionaires, they do not know how to invest, they are struggling financially, and so on. The audience is made to feel more helpless and stupid as they realise that the presenter has achieved what they want, and the audience is therefore tricked into trusting the presenter to help them realise their dreams. The corporate criminal psychopath suggests to the audience that it takes courage and determination and trust to invest in their 'scheme' – the reverse psychology stage. The audience is then influenced to prove their trust by investing their money in the 'scheme'. At this point, the corporate criminal psychopath either sells the victims over-inflated 'investment packages' or takes their money and disappears.

Identity theft and the corporate criminal psychopath

Albert had worked all his life as an accountant. He hated the daily grind of his nine to five office job, and looked forward to his retirement. Finally, at fifty he could afford to retire and live off the dividends he received from his blue-chip shares. Albert moved up to Queensland with his wife, and they looked forward to enjoying themselves in complete financial security.

Robert was a corporate criminal psychopath who 'happened' to use the ATM after Albert made a withdrawal. Robert used to watch the ATM for wealthy retirees. From Albert's discarded ATM slip, Robert got Albert's name, account number and account balance. Robert also followed Albert home and was able to steal an electricity bill from Albert's letterbox. Using the electricity bill and a forged birth certificate as proof of identity, Robert organised a new Medicare card to be sent to 'Albert' care of Robert's post office box. Robert then opened a bank account in Albert's name.

When Robert was going though Albert's mail, he noticed a letter from Albert's stockbroker. This letter revealed detailed information about Albert's shares and investments. Robert contacted Albert's stockbroker, pretending to be Albert, and presented the false driver's licence and other forms of identification, organising Albert's stocks to be linked to the false bank account he had set up in Albert's name. Robert also changed Albert's password for buying and selling shares, and sold all of Albert's shares and had the proceeds of the sale deposited into the false bank account. Robert then withdrew the money, via an overseas bank, and disappeared.

Albert had no idea any of this had happened until, worried because his dividend cheques were taking longer than usual to arrive in the post, he contacted his stockbroker. At first his stockbroker would not reveal any information to him, as Albert did not know the new account password. Eventually Albert discovered that all his shares had been sold.

Albert is working again, in a position much lower than he once held, as he still has to earn enough money to support himself and his wife and to make the final payments on his retirement home. He felt like his entire life's work had been stolen from him.

One of the fastest growing organised crimes in the twenty-first century is identity theft. This particular crime involves a criminal assuming someone else's identity and using it to make purchases on credit, apply for loans, buy cars, commit crime, and withdraw money from the victim's bank accounts.

Given their personality characteristics, it is relatively simple for the corporate criminal psychopath to steal a person's identity. They are glib and superficial, making it easy to pretend they are someone else, and they have no remorse or guilt so they do not seem suspicious. In relation to the psychopathy characteristics, they often spend the money on fast cars, parties, gambling, drugs, and women. Being prone to boredom is also a motivating factor, as is the need for excitement in actually getting away with this type of fraud.

Other corporate criminal psychopaths use stolen identities to get jobs in companies from which they steal information or money. The corporate criminal psychopath who steals someone else's identity is not worried about being caught at all as they know that if their fraud is detected, they are able to disappear at will. Some of these offenders steal information from companies and sell it to other rival companies, others sell information to organised criminals about security arrangements in the victim's company. It is not un-common for these offenders to go through corporate files and record details of customers so that they have a ready supply of information necessary to steal another identity if they need to. This personal information is also sold, usually over the Internet, to allow other corporate criminal psychopaths to become someone else. A final group of 'identity' offenders simply steal funds from a corporation, and when the theft is detected, they disappear withdrawing all the money from the false account as cash, which is then moved overseas and transferred into some other form of untraceable investment such as gold, antiques, paintings, illegal drugs, and so on.

One final interesting use of 'borrowing' a person's identity is for money laundering. Suppose a corporate criminal psychopath has $20,000 as a result of a white-collar crime, and they do not want to put this money in the bank as they cannot prove to investigators that it is not the proceeds of illegal activity. One way of 'borrowing' a person's identity is to go to a casino and wait for someone to win say $18,000. This person is given a ticket that allows them to collect their prize when they leave the casino. The corporate criminal psychopath in question may approach the 'winner' and offer to buy the $18,000 winning ticket for $20,000. The innocent winner agrees to this, as they gain $2000 more than their winnings for the exchange. The psychopath then cashes the winning ticket in their own name, and there is then a legitimate record for where they obtained $18,000.

Real estate property theft is another avenue the corporate criminal psychopath and organised crime syndicates use to fraudulently obtain large amounts of money. The scheme is quite simple. The corporate criminal psychopath uses forged title deeds to steal large sums of money from mortgage lenders. Basically, the corporate criminal psychopath will present the forged title deeds to a lender and ask for a loan using 'their' property as security. They will open an account in a false name to deposit their funds. Once the funds are deposited, they are quickly withdrawn from over-seas branches of the bank and the person who took out the loan disappears.

The corporate criminal psychopath commits a number of types of fraud; white-collar crime, blue-collar workers stealing from their employers, self-employed con-artists and organised crime figures. This type of psychopath is equally likely to be male or female, young or old, upper, middle or lower class. The cor-porate criminal psychopath is able to blend into the organisation or society so well it often is difficult to detect them until it is too late.

6

THE VIOLENT CRIMINAL PSYCHOPATH

ALI WAS A thirty-year-old mobile security guard responsible for patrolling a suburban neighbourhood late at night. He was very proud of his job, and had caught quite a few people breaking into houses or damaging other people's property. He was licensed to carry a pistol, baton and handcuffs. Over the years, he had grown very familiar with his patrol area, knew the people living there and the streets very well. He was regarded as friendly and professional by his colleagues, and had appeared in court on many occasions to testify against offenders he had apprehended. Ali felt powerful when he 'arrested' people, particularly young males. It made him feel important to testify against them in court.

It was 3 a.m. and twenty-two-year-old Charles was in an unfamiliar neighbourhood, with no money, waiting for a passing car to catch a ride to the railway station. He had been to a party with some friends and was slightly drunk. A car pulled up and to his relief it was a security guard, someone who could be trusted. The security guard told him to get in, he could give him a lift.

Ali could not believe his luck. Ali was a sadistic homosexual rapist who had sexually assaulted a number of other young men he had kidnapped while patrolling the residential area as a security guard. He used his job as an opportunity to pick-up victims late at night, kidnapping them with little resistance. He would use the tools of his trade to restrain and then maintain control over his victims.

Charles realised something was wrong after being driven around the back streets for over 15 minutes. He asked the security guard where they were going. At this point, Ali became very angry, pointed his gun at Charles and told him to get on the floor of the car so he could not be seen from outside. Ali drove around for another 40 minutes, finishing up the patrol of the area. Ali would have felt a mounting excitement as he thought about what he was going to do to Charles. He would also have felt very powerful as Charles became increasingly terrified when he realised that something terrible was going to happen to him. Charles did not move because he truly believed that Ali would shoot him if he resisted in any way.

Ali took Charles to his house, where he sadistically sexually assaulted him for a prolonged period of time. Ali also videotaped the sexual assaults so that he could relive the assaults over and over again after he had released his victim. The things Ali did to Charles are too sadistic to describe in detail here. One behaviour was Ali's use of his security baton to penetrate his victims anally and orally. Every time he saw his baton it was a reminder of the deviant behaviours he had committed. Ali was an individual committing very serious crimes, yet people saw him as a trusted member of society there to protect them.

Ali sexually assaulted a number of young males while on duty. Each sexual assault became more sadistic than the last. At the time of his arrest, paperwork was found in his house indicating that he was going to apply to the police force. Given that he had no criminal record, could have probably passed the personality tests and was a good talker, it is likely he would have been accepted as a police officer.

The violent criminal psychopath can be found working in a variety of professions. Some use their position to find victims, while others do their job as a means of making money and supporting themselves and, quite often, a family.

The violent criminal psychopath is not violent all day, every day. They do not appear different from everyone else when you look at or talk to them. While not all violent criminals are psychopaths a large proportion are. This is particularly true for recidivist violent offenders or offenders who repeatedly commit a crime. The violent criminal psychopath is also likely to be involved in many types of crime, both violent and non-violent. Not all of them are caught for these crimes, so not all of them have extensive criminal records. In fact, some of them have no criminal record at all until they are caught for a major offence.

Homicide

People kill each other for many reasons. Jealousy, lust, revenge, hatred, enjoyment, alcohol, drugs and money are just a few explanations. Many murderers do not necessarily fit the criteria for being violent criminal psychopaths. In Australia, most murders are committed by someone known to the victim, usually a close family member or friend. In many of these murders, the offender loses control of themselves (often under the influence of drugs and/or alcohol) and acts on impulse. While this doesn't excuse their behaviour, it does not make them psychopathic. Often they regret their behaviours, and they do not show sufficient characteristics for a diagnosis of psychopathy.

Then there are the homicide offenders who are violent criminal psychopaths. Generally these people kill and feel no remorse for their behaviours. Four main motivations exist for their murders – power, anger, sex, and money. The first three of these four motivations are often linked together. Money can be the catalyst for a homicide on its own.

Contract killer

A contract killer is someone who agrees to take the life of another person for profit. There is usually an absence of any relationship between the killer and the victim. The contract killer is relevant to violent criminal psychopaths found in the workplace because business partners, co-workers and clients have all been known to 'take out a contract' to murder someone they know through work. Often the victim is seen as a business rival or a hindrance to some business or personal financial plan.

Generally, a contract killer spends a significant amount of time observing their victim, becoming familiar with their movement patterns and schedule. They are methodical, experienced in other types of violent crime and plan the 'hit' carefully. The murder itself is usually quick with little evidence left at the crime scene. The successful hitman has higher intelligence and devotes more time to planning the crime than their less successful counterparts who are often caught.

It is easier for a psychopathic co-worker, employee, or boss with pre-existing criminal connections to take out a contract on someone. The colleague who takes out this contract will often contact the killer (a violent criminal psychopath), as evidenced by telephone records, mail records, email, etc. The contractor will usually have a history of personal conflict or business competition with the victim. However, the contractor (person engaging the killer) will often show an improvement in relationship with the victim prior to the murder. This is often very deliberately done in front of relatives, friends, and business associates. This is to lure the victim into a false sense of security while convincing those around him that he is above suspicion. After the murder has taken place, the contractor will often have an unusually detailed 'memory' of where they were at the exact time the victim was killed. Precise times will often be remembered (supported by receipts, alibis etc) but actions during the time period preceding and following the offence will be recalled less accurately.

Specific financial indicators can point to a financial motive for taking a contract out on a person. Numerous bank accounts, increased borrowing of funds, dishonoured cheques, over-insured assets, frequent losses in previous years, multiple insurance claims, large or overdue accounts payable, costly lease or rental agreements, credit restrictions on credit cards and unprofitable contracts are all potential indicators of a financial need to eliminate another person for business reasons.

When these financial aspects are combined with the psychopathy characteristics described in Chapter 2, and a business or personal rival is murdered or dies 'accidentally', it is possible that a contract hit has been organised. Contracts have been taken out on people from a wide variety of professions and walks of life, such as police officers, landlords, tenants, rival drug dealers, lawyers, insurance agents, judges, partners, children, parents, and wealthy relatives to name but a few.

Sexual homicide

A sexual homicide is a homicide in which the offender performs some type of sexual behaviour before, during, or after the homicide has taken place. This does not have to be a sexual act with the victim. It can be an autoerotic activity such as masturbation or a sexual substitution activity such as stabbing the dead victim. Victims of sexual homicide include strangers and people known to the offender. These victims can include people met through their work, or even colleagues.

Generally a sexual homicide offender kills a victim to feel powerful. The killer controls what the victim does, and ultimately they control when and how the victim dies. When this feeling of power and control are combined with a sexual climax reported by one offender to be 'the biggest high you can imagine' it leads to repeated or serial murders, as the offender seeks this positive feeling again and again. At the same time, the sexual homicide is shaped by the offender's sexual fantasies. The actual sexual homicide is never as good as what the offender fantasises about, therefore they continue to kill in a futile attempt to have the act of murder as good as or better than their fantasy.

The FBI divide sexual homicide offenders into two groups – organised and disorganised killers. The disorganised offender is not always a violent criminal psychopath. Some of them are motivated by mental illness. However, many of the disorganised violent criminal psychopaths attempt to convince the legal system that they are mentally ill to escape punishment for their crimes. The disorganised offender most likely lives alone or with a parental figure. They usually live or work close to the crime scene. Work performance is generally inconsistent or poor, with frequent job changes. Often they have inferior social skills, and if they are in a relationship it is usually with someone much older or younger.

Following is an example of a violent criminal

psychopath using his workplace to capture and murder a female victim in a large Australian city in the 1990s.

> [His] victim was found rolled in a rug in a lane outside the delivery area of a commercial building in the city. Crime scene investigators found a female who had extensive mutilation to her face and body. The fingers of the victim had been removed, and a series of intricate patterns had been carved into the victim's stomach. There were ligature marks on her wrists and ankles. When the post-mortem had been completed, it was discovered that the female had been orally, anally and vaginally sexually assaulted, and had obviously been restrained throughout the assault. Death was caused by ligature strangulation.

The violent criminal psychopath in this particular example was a security guard of average intelligence who worked at the front desk in the female victim's high-rise office building. The security guard had ingratiated himself with the victim by walking her to her car after work on many nights leading up to her murder – he made her feel safe with him. Unknown to her, he had been hiding his dark thoughts and fantasies about her – ritualistically killing her combined with inhumane sexual acts – the 'trusted' security guard would have complete control over his unsuspecting victim. Absolute control was exerted not only during her struggle to survive the brutal attack, but also when he mutilated her body after her death. This example of a violent criminal psychopath shows how sexual homicide offenders are able to use with chilling effect the trust gained through their position at work to abduct and murder their victims.

The organised sexual homicide offender is generally of above average intelligence, has good social skills, prefers to do skilled work, frequently lives with a partner, has a car and often leaves their job or takes some time off work immediately after committing a murder. They are often irritable before committing a murder, and may use alcohol or drugs to give them confidence.

Sexual assault

There are four main types of stranger rapist – the power-assertive, the power-reassurance, the anger-retaliatory, the anger-excitation – each type is driven by unique psychological factors that cause variation in both sexual assault behaviour and victim selection. Each type of rapist is also likely to be found in a wide range of work environments because of their distinctive personality types.

Most sexual assaults are committed by someone the victims knows. This includes partners, dates, friends, relatives, work colleagues. These individuals are often motivated by a sense of entitlement to have sex with the victim, or easy access to a vulnerable sexual partner. These rapists can be found in a wide variety of professions and workplaces, ranging from professionals to the long-term unemployed.

The first type of stranger rapist is the power-assertive offender. These offenders sexually assault as an expression of their macho image. This type of rapist is also driven by the thrill of control and domination. They believe that any woman would be grateful to have sex with them. Moreover, this type of rapist believes that he is entitled to have sex with whoever he wants because he is a 'man'. Often their victim is a stranger who is forced rather than conned into going with the offender. The victim is frequently beaten, but only to ensure they comply with the offender's demands. The offender may also use a weapon to threaten the victim. The power-assertive offender will not engage in 'perverse' sexual acts as he (Masculine gender is used here as it is predominantly men who are classified using these criteria. Research on female sex offenders who rape other adults is rare.) sees this as deviant behaviour.

The power-assertive offender often starts in their late teens to mid-twenties, and is described as 'emotionally primitive'. They are predominantly concerned with projecting a macho image, and live their lives accordingly. Physical fitness and other activity designed to portray a 'tough' exterior are important to these offenders. They are arrogant, egocentric and grandiose, treating other people as less important than themselves. They are prone to boredom, impulsive on occasion, and will use alcohol and/or drugs, but not to the point of losing control over themselves. While they may associate with other people, usually men similar to or seen as inferior to themselves, they are not viewed as a 'team player'. They may have been married on more than one occasion, and have affairs with consenting adult partners. Their sexual behaviour is selfish. They often dropout of high school, and their work history is sporadic as they frequently have problems with authority figures in their work environments. They generally fit in with the people they work with, but managers would see them as 'difficult employees' because it is clear to everyone that they are 'out for themselves'. They generally alternate between receiving unemployment benefits and doing outdoor type jobs that involve manual labour, consistent with their projected macho image. Their case workers report that they are difficult to place in jobs given their attitude toward work and authority figures.

The second type of rapist is the power-reassurance offender. This rapist sexually assaults because he believes the woman will enjoy the sexual experience, reinforcing a false self-belief that he is a powerful, virile male able to sexually satisfy whomever he chooses. Sexuality is essentially an expression of conquest. The characteristic scenario in the power-reassurance rapist's mind is one in which the victim initially resists their sexual advances but once she is overpowered, the victim cannot resist her assailant's sexual prowess and becomes sexually aroused and receptive to his embrace. Often these offenders will make their victims ask for sexual acts to be performed, tell them what a good lover they are, compare the offender to their boyfriend/husband, simulate sexual arousal and orgasm, and so on. This rapist typically has a high degree of self-importance and unrealistic fantasies about relationships.

Throughout the attack, the offender uses only the amount of force necessary to capture and control his victim. He may achieve this through using verbal threats (Do what I say and I won't hurt you), or intimidation with a weapon (I came up behind her and put a knife to her throat and told her to come with me), and/or physical force (I told her to undress, and when she refused I hit her in the face to show her I meant business).

Maria woke up at 3 a.m. because she felt something wet on her chest. At first she thought it was a dream, but gradually realised that the man she had seen in the lift at work over the past few weeks was kneeling over her as she slept in her bed. He was licking her breast and caressing her leg. The man had broken in and was watching her sleep until he could not restrain himself from touching and kissing her. He told her to relax, that he would do all the work and that he loved her.

A shocked Maria calmly asked him what he was doing, and he stopped as though he could not understand why she would ask such a ridiculous question. He showed her a knife, and sat next to her on the bed, running his fingers through her hair as he explained that he knew she wanted it. He told her to kiss him on the mouth and fondle his penis. Maria did as she feared for her life. She also tried to stall him by saying that she wanted some alcohol, but she had run out. The man left the house to buy some alcohol and Maria called the police. The man was arrested as he was driving back to her house. He genuinely believed that she wanted to have sex with him, as this was what he had fantasised about while he had watched her at work.

The offender worked in the same company as Maria, and had been watching her for a considerable period of time. When a search warrant was executed on his house, he had diaries detailing Maria's movements, drawings of her, and writings about how it would make him and her feel when they were finally able to 'make love' to each other. The company that employed him was not aware he had prior convictions for sexual offences, stealing and breaking into people's houses.

The third type of rapist is the anger-retaliatory or anger-hostility rapist. These offenders punish and degrade women by sexually assaulting them, in effect symbolically destroying them in response to their hatred of women in general. Anger is a fundamental component of this offender's motivation.

The anger-retaliatory rapist will use extreme levels of force, far more than is necessary, to control the victim. This is a direct result of the tumultuous emotional state of the offender. There is frequently a triggering event in the offender's life that initiates the sexual assault. This can include a fight with a female figure in their lives (boss, co-worker, wife, girlfriend, mother, daughter); feeling dominated by a female person, a court date, losing their job, car accident, neighbour complaints about them, the list is endless.

Generally the attack is very sudden, the victim is subdued by extreme force, denying her any opportunity to defend herself. FBI profiler Roy Hazelwood in his book *Dark Dreams* has identified that this offender typically attacks women of a similar age or older than themselves. Weapons of opportunity are used, most commonly fists and feet. Attacks are sporadic, as they depend on stressful events that lead up to sufficient anger to propel the offender to commit another sexual assault.

Neil was a thirty-year-old male who worked in a number of short-term manual labour type jobs. These included handyman, gardener, factory worker, and furniture removalist. He had been fired from each of these jobs as he failed to turn up or did not do enough work. One employer recalled that Neil was a favourite with the elderly residents when he was working as a gardener for nursing homes and private residents. He would often help out elderly ladies by moving furniture around and tidying their outdoor areas for no charge. He was very outgoing and eager to please. Neil's female de-facto partner described him as a nice man, someone who would do anything to help out a friend. Interestingly, she also remarked that she had to 'keep him in line' sometimes, particularly when it came to doing work around the house.

Two days after Neil had a fight with his partner, he broke into the house of an elderly lady. He pulled her out of bed, beat her around the face and chest, and forced her to perform a variety of sexual acts. His victim was hospitalised for a number of weeks, and at one stage it looked as though she was going to die as a result of her injuries. This assault was one of a number Neil was responsible for, and each assault escalated in terms of violence and sexual acts performed. Prior to each assault, Neil had either had a fight with his partner, had a court date coming up for an assault matter, had a fight with his neighbours, or been kicked out by one of his girl-friends. Neil said he assaulted the women because he hated them, he wanted to destroy them. Women were always telling him what to do and, according to him, his grandmother, in particular, was a real tyrant. Neil was destroying people who represented his grandmother by using sex as a weapon.

The final type of rapist is the anger-excitation or sadistic rapist. This rapist differs from the others as they are sexually stimulated by their victim's response to emotional and physical pain. These offenders plan and execute their crimes with extreme precision. Weapons and instruments, transportation, travel routes, record-ing devices, and bindings are all pre-planned. The victim is usually a targeted stranger. This is because this rapist is the most intelligent of all rapists, and they want no ties that can link them to the victim. Most often they use the 'con approach', luring their victim into the right situation for the sexual assault to occur. After gaining the victim's confidence, they are quickly immobilised and transported to a pre-selected location. The assault usually involves bondage and torture, and frequently has a bizarre or ritualistic quality to it.

In terms of employment, the sadistic offender may

move frequently between jobs until he finds a position that has minimum supervision. Given their precise nature as reflected in their crimes, they may also show a preference for mechanical or manual jobs such as building, carpentry, specialty factory worker, machine operator. Given the intelligence of some offenders, they may also have jobs as accountants, auditors, specialist managers, specialist lawyers, scientists, and other professions that require meticulousness. It is not uncommon for the sadistic offender to be university educated.

The sadistic offender generally has good social skills, glib and superficial charm and a manner that allows them to lull victims into a false sense of security. They appear to be law-abiding citizens, a façade that is used to deceive people in their lives. They are often married, and their partners report they suspected nothing. The offender appears to be a loyal and conservative husband. Financially they are often adequate providers. One interesting aspect of the sadistic offender is their tendency to act out with willing sexual partners such as compliant wives, girlfriends or prostitutes. They are also avid collectors of pornography associated with their sexual preference, and they frequently keep items stolen from victims as a souvenir or trophy of each sexual assault. The first case study of Ali is an example of a sadistic rapist.

Child molesters – paedophilia
Paedophiles are generally classified as one of two types; fixated or situational/regressed. The fixated paedophile

is primarily sexually aroused by having sex with children. They are often in positions that allow them to access children, such as childcare, teaching, employers of adolescents, leading youth groups, priests, music teachers, youth workers, sports coaches. They carefully plan their assaults, grooming the children to perform more and more sexual behaviours, though they have also been known to abduct child victims. They invest great amounts of time, effort and money, into gaining access to children, often giving away expensive computer games, drugs, money taking the children out, and so on. Some fixated paedophiles have even been known to employ children and then sexually abuse them at work. They are very unlikely to change their behaviour, portraying themselves as 'model' citizens. They are usually above average intelligence, and have good social skills. Friends and colleagues are often surprised when these types of paedophiles are discovered, and often continue to support them. It is not unknown for these offenders to marry into a 'ready made' family where they have access to children.

Tony was the owner of a contract cleaning firm that was responsible for daily maintenance of office buildings, as well as home and garden maintenance for private clients. It was a very successful business with a good reputation for reliability and honesty. Tony could not keep up with the work that was coming in and decided to hire some young men, paying them cash. Tony had a good friend, Max, who he had known for a couple of years and met through an Internet site. Being a youth worker at a

> refuge, Max was able to hand over vulnerable young boys
> to help Tony out with his business. Tony would offer the
> boys a job, then extra money for sex and photographs.

With easy access to the Internet, collecting child pornography from the privacy of the home or office has become significantly easier for the fixated paedophile. The majority of paedophiles who act out their fantasies also collect child pornography.

The situational or regressed paedophile is primarily sexually attracted to consenting adults. Their sexual interest in children generally emerges in adulthood. They sexually assault children as a means of coping with a stressful situation in their lives. The initial assault may be impulsive, though later offences are often premeditated. This type of offence is all about power and control. In essence, the offender has a situation in life they cannot resolve or cope with, therefore they feel as though they have lost control over themselves. In their mind, one of the easiest things to control is a child, so they sexually assault a child to feel powerful. It is common for alcohol use to be associated with the offence, and a noticeable change in the offender's work behaviour often occurs after an assault. They may not turn up for work, appear distracted, or be withdrawn from the people around them. Alcohol and/or drug use after a crime may also increase.

Arson

Over the past few decades Australian suburbs have been ravaged by bushfires. Although weather and bushland conditions have been a contributing factor, investigations reveal that some of these fires have been deliberately lit by firefighters working amongst those who were trying to save lives and property, such as this case reported in the *Manly Daily*:

> *A Rural Fire Service probationary trainee firefighter was charged with lighting a bushfire that ravaged more than 1400 ha of National Park. The twenty-three-year-old male was charged with three counts of arson, in addition to illegally using a stolen boat. The bushfire burned for five days threatening homes, and required hundreds of volunteer firefighters from across Sydney.*

Other examples of arsonists in the workplace include revenge motivated arsonists, who target their workplace or colleagues possessions; or insurance-related arson attacks with money and profit being the motivating factor. While not all arsonists are violent criminal psychopaths, a large proportion of them have very similar characteristics to other types of psychopaths.

One of the most common motivators for arson is excitement. An excitement-motivated arson happens when a person is thrilled by the act of starting a fire, and is also stimulated seeing the fire put out. The thrill seems to be centred around the power the fire gives the arsonist, or the attention they get from the effect of the fire. One volunteer firefighter told police that he got emotional satisfaction from the praise heaped on volunteer firefighters. He lit fires because he was bored as well as getting a feeling of accomplishment. He would ring to report the fires he had lit, and was usually the first one at the scene to put them out. Another professional firefighter was responsible for over thirty fires. He also had a history of firearms offences, drink driving, malicious damage, and stealing. Some of the fires he lit were revenge motivated, while others were excitement motivated. Again, he would notify '000' and then attend to put the fire out.

Revenge-motivated arson is where a fire is lit as a reaction to a person's or organisation's behaviour. The violent criminal psychopath may set fire to their workplace, or machinery in their workplace, to gain time off or because their employer has 'done something' to them. Revenge arson can be directed towards employers, other co-workers, domestic dispute targets, teachers, neighbours, government organisations, etc. These types of arsonists are generally adult males with ten or more years of education and work in a non-professional position. According to the profile of the arsonist, they generally live in lower-level socio-economic areas and do not maintain long-term relationships.

Vandalism-motivated arson is often directed at educational facilities and vegetation/bins etc. The offenders are usually not violent criminal psychopaths, instead they are most often juvenile males with seven to nine years of schooling. They usually live 1–2 km from the school premises. They are frequently seen around the school before the fire, and may graffiti areas around the school. They return home very soon after lighting the fire to escape detection. Often they have a history of being troublemakers in the school they set fire to.

Profit-motivated arson involves setting fire to a structure for money. It is usually well planned, with specific targets. Indicators are an excessive use of accelerants and lack of forced entry. Insurance is the major reason for profit motivated arson, and major targets are commercial premises and motor vehicles. The NSW Bureau of Crime Statistics and Research report that arson for profit is usually not committed by the recipient of the fraud, but by a paid arsonist who usually has prior criminal convictions. This paid arsonist is often a criminal psychopath who will destroy property without regard for the consequences for other people.

The violent criminal psychopath is important when talking about psychopaths in the workplace for two reasons. First, the various types of violent criminal psychopath sometimes select their victims from the people they work with or encounter through their work. Second, people may work unknowingly with a violent criminal psychopath. The violent criminal psychopath does not stand out as an obvious 'psychopath' or monster, so it is important to be familiar with this type of psychopath who can be found in a variety of workplaces.

7

THE OCCUPATIONAL PSYCHOPATH

THE OCCUPATIONAL PSYCHOPATH is someone who uses their job or profession to indulge in the need for power and control. Usually the jobs that they take also puts them in a position where they can legitimately exert power and control. Police work, parking officers and security guards can be perfect covers for these types of psychopaths.

Characteristically, the occupational psychopath desires power and control but does not feel comfortable with conflict. They hide behind the power their job brings them. Alternatively, these types are excellent manipulators who use their jobs to trap their victims in a web of deceit without the victim realising what is happening.

The occupational psychopath can generally be classified as one of two types based on the type of victim they choose. The first type is the occupational psychopath – generalised victim type; the second is the occupational psychopath – targeted victim type.

Generalised victim type

The occupational psychopath – generalised victim type doesn't discriminate. They are prepared to exploit anyone they come across as long as they can avoid being caught out. An example of this is a police officer who intimidates, manipulates or assaults people randomly as they come into contact with them through the nature of their work.

James was a twenty-eight year old policeman working in Highway Patrol. He appeared to love his job as he rarely talked about anything else. James loved the idea of handing out traffic tickets so much that he would write them out even if no offence was committed. He enjoyed writing out tickets that were worth up to one month's wages, knowing there was nothing that the person receiving the ticket could do about it. He abused his position of trust in a number of ways which made him feel powerful.

James lived alone in a unit crammed with police equipment. He had stolen police stationery, badges, uniforms and files containing sensitive information. He even had a set of emergency police lights set up in his bedroom. James drove a car that was identical to his highway patrol vehicle. In the car he had a police scanner, as well as a blue flashing light similar to those used by detectives and undercover police. It is not known if James pulled people over using his personal vehicle, however it seems likely given his personality. All of these items reminded James of what a powerful person he was, how he was able to do what he wanted, including breaking the law, without getting caught.

James had more complaints made against him than any other officer in his area. They ranged from allegations that he had assaulted prisoners to swearing at members of the public, using his firearm when it was not warranted, and ignoring requests to attend serious crimes because he did not feel like attending. As a result, his colleagues felt he was a danger to them and to members of the public. However, James was always able to provide an explanation for his behaviour that satisfied the departmental guidelines, therefore no disciplinary action could be taken. James did not accept guidance from anyone, and he never appeared to be sorry for anything he did.

A camera was installed in James' highway patrol car (with his knowledge) after numerous complaints had been received about his behaviour. On one occasion, James was seen to pull over a couple for speeding. He requested a vehicle check. It turned out the drivers had no criminal record. Despite this, James pulled out his firearm and coldly asked the couple to step out of the car slowly, while he aimed his firearm at them. James' behaviour made the couple feel uneasy, as though if they didn't do what he asked them to he would shoot them. When asked to justify his behaviour, James said it was a judgment call that made him take such action, something did not feel right to him about the vehicle and its occupants. This was an obvious lie, but couldn't be proven, so no action was taken against him. His victims were returning from a holiday. Their only crime was to exceed the speed limit by 10 km/ph.

James would also bully and manipulate colleagues into covering up his behaviour, particularly younger police officers because they saw James as 'gung-ho' when they first met him. For some he was a role model, until they saw how deceitful he was. James told one colleague he was quite proud of his ability to play the system.

James was eventually put on restricted duties (that is, working at a desk job in the police station) after one too many complaints had been received about him. Characteristically, he quickly became bored with his new duties and resigned from the police force. He joined a security firm as a patrol officer for a high-crime residential neighbourhood.

The occupational psychopath – generalised victim type is often good at explaining their behaviour when they are caught for 'going too far'. It is common for them to promise that they won't behave like that again, it wasn't their fault – anything to divert attention away from themselves and to avoid conflict. They make excuses for their behaviour with conviction and sincerity, making sure others believe them. This type of occupational psychopath will work even harder to hide their behaviour and aim to prove to others that they are responsible, not a difficult employee at all. Concealing behaviour buys time to refine their victimisation strategies and minimise their chances of being caught again.

Tactics and strategies

The occupational psychopath – generalised victim type goes through a number of stages from when they enter an organisation. These stages are similar to those used by the organisational and corporate criminal psychopaths.

First, they evaluate their colleagues and the rules of the organisation they are working for. The organisation is often a government agency, or some type of institution whereby their position comes with legislated or implicit power and authority over other people. In the early stages when they join the organisation, they assess what self-gratifying behaviours will and will not be detected by existing supervision systems. They also evaluate their co-workers' psychological weaknesses in case they ever need to exploit them in the future. To the people around them, the occupational psychopath appears eager to learn and enthusiastic about their job in the early stages of their employment.

Second, is that along with manipulating people and work systems to their personal advantage, avoiding close supervision, they gradually begin to break very minor rules so that people become used to their 'idiosyncrasies'. They are getting their colleagues used to their rule 'bending' behaviour. If a supervisor does notice a rule violation, the occupational psychopath will promise never to break the rule again and plead ignorance of its existence as 'they are new here' or 'they have never been told, but now they know it will not happen again'. The occupational psychopath also shows a preference for tasks or jobs that can be performed alone. This provides them with the opportunity to victimise people they come into contact with through their work without being detected.

Third, the occupational psychopath establishes a system that allows the occupational psychopath to cover their behaviours by being extremely knowledgeable about the regulations they work under. They research their responsibilities, and develop plausible sounding explanations for when complaints are made against them by co-workers or members of the public. These types pride themselves on covering up any trace of their crimes.

Bob was a social worker responsible for looking after the needs of homeless youth in the inner city. Instead, Bob was running an organised ring of thieves made up of the youth he was supposed to look after. His work suffered because he did not have the time to both perform social work duties and run a crime ring. Eventually another social worker discovered what Bob was doing. Bob had covered his role in the crime ring so well that he could never be charged.

This type of psychopath behaves more cautiously than the other sub-types – they will work out how far they can push workplace boundaries. They start by targeting one or two victims, gradually increasing the number of victims, until they are eventually caught. Because they are so good at hiding their deceitful behaviours the organisational psychopath will either leave an organisation before action against them is taken, or they will cleverly make 'the complaint' disappear through subtle intimidation.

Targeted victim type

Michael, a doctor, had set himself up as a 'spiritual healer and counsellor'. Over the years he had recruited a number of female clients to live with him at a 'spiritual retreat' – an isolated community in a semi-rural area. Michael provided 'therapy' and the women were coerced into providing sexual favours, recruiting new therapy group members and financing the operation by handing over their wages and savings. In return Michael promised happiness and security.

Michael would play on his clients' insecurities to recruit them and encouraged the severing of ties with family and friends. Michael also claimed that family and friends were the cause of insecurity and loneliness, and needed to be cut out of a person's life to achieve happiness. In reality, this was to eliminate an independent voice of reason that his victims could talk to when they had doubts about Michael's methods. He made sure his victims were always too emotionally involved in a situation to think clearly about what they were doing.

In order to attract women to his 'spiritual retreat', Michael would use a 'soft-sell' approach appealing to women with low self-esteem and promoting exclusive membership. If anyone turned down an offer to join, it was implied that the person was stupid for passing up on such an opportunity.

To keep these women 'under control', Michael would continue to exploit their particular feelings of loneliness and insecurity. He would use 'therapy sessions' to reinforce these feelings which would then make these women dependent on him to help them in their search for happiness and companionship.

Michael also revealed an abusive streak – he did not tolerate criticism from anyone and often flew into irrational rages. This was all part of his strategy to keep control of the women by intimidating them with his volatile behaviour. He would claim it was difficult to guide such a troubled group of women, and they should be thankful he stayed with them rather than focus on his anger and frustration.

Sex was used as a power and control tactic by Michael, who would sleep with all of the women who came through the retreat. Because of the power imbalance between Michael and his followers, the sexual contact was not truly consensual which had damaging consequences.

The occupational psychopath – targeted victim type identifies specific vulnerable people and uses professional knowledge and work-related skills to exploit their victims. These psychopaths are often found in white-collar professions in positions of trust and responsibility – teachers, psychologists, doctors, counsellors. They have above-average intelligence and have a deep understanding of other people's thought processes and emotional states. They use this understanding to exploit their victim's weak points and insecurities.

Victims targeted by this type of occupational psychopath can be divided into three categories. The first group are brought together as a group by the psychopath and exploited *en masse*. This group is used to satisfy the psychopath's self-gratification needs such as sex, power and control. A 'cult' is an example of this. However, not all cult leaders are psychopaths.

The second targeted group of victims are systematically exploited by the occupational psychopath one at a time, the victim doesn't know there are other victims. For example, a psychiatrist who is an occupational psychopath may manipulate a number of patients into fulfilling him sexually. These patients would not be aware of each other's existence as the psychopath never allows them to meet.

The final targeted group of victims are exploited one after another. For example, a psychologist may manipulate a patient into signing over large sums of money to them for worthless 'therapy programs', and when one client has been 'bled dry', will move on to another vulnerable victim.

Methods used to recruit and exploit victims are essentially the same, regardless of how many victims are exploited and whether they know each other. The psychopath who exploits a group of victims that interact with one another requires a greater understanding of group processes than other occupational psychopaths with different target victims. However, the underlying principles of exploitation, power and control are the same.

Tactics and strategies

The occupational psychopath – targeted victim type uses a number of stages to gratify their selfish needs at the expense of their victims. This is true of the psychopath who targets and recruits groups of victims, such as a cult leader, as well as those who target and exploit one victim at a time.

- *Selecting a victim* – It is a common misconception that victims who fall prey to the occupational psychopath are unstable, weird or are of low intelligence. Occupational psychopaths who recruit group members for 'cult'-like groups tend to search out intelligent people who are productive, energetic and active so that they will raise funds for the cult, lend it an air of respectability, recruit new members, and operate 'group-owned' businesses. Occupational psychopaths who exploit individuals separately are not as stringent in their victim requirements. They seek a person who is obviously susceptible to the manipulative approach. As with other sub-types and their victims, the key factors are vulnerability, low self-esteem, the desire to change and a yearning for a better life.

- *Establishing total control* – The occupational psychopath puts a system in place so they can control their victim's behaviour completely. This control is gained through 'breaking' the person's personality. Making the victim fearful is the first step. This creation of fear in the victim is usually disguised as a concern for their welfare. For example, an occupational psychopath may emphasise the terrible fate in store for people who disobey him or her. This is tempered with the pretence of concern. In reality, the victim is made aware of the negative consequences of questioning or going against the occupational psychopath. Subconsciously the foundations of fear of disobeying are laid down. Once fear is established, the occupational psychopath has control over the victim. From this point it is just a matter of maintaining that fear and control.

- *The 'code of silence'* – To be able to continue controlling their victim, the occupational psychopath needs to guarantee the victim's silence so that their psychopathic behaviour can continue undetected. This can be done by telling the victim that if they talk to anyone else about what is happening, they will ruin any chances they have of achieving what they want in life. This isolates the victim from any help or support as they push everyone who is close to them away. At the same time, the occupational psychopath is continually destroying their self-esteem, until the victim feels as though the occupational psychopath is the only person they can trust and depend on in their life.

Occupational psychopath – a unique sub-type?

The occupational psychopath shares characteristics with each of the other three sub-types of psychopath found in the workplace. Some occupational psychopaths perform violent and/or non-violent criminal behaviours, others manipulate people in their workplace to escape detection for their psychopathic behaviours.

Paulo, a Brazilian policeman was an occupational psychopath and provides an example of the crossover between the occupational psychopath and each of the other workplace psychopath sub-types – organisational, corporate criminal and violent criminal psychopaths.

The favela district of Rio de Janeiro, Brazil, a slum area controlled by drug cartels, was created by hundreds of thousands of people from rural areas moving to the city for work. People arrived to find that work was either non-existent or very poorly paid, and they were forced to live on the outskirts of the cities in shantytowns. The favelas, or shantytowns, in Rio are now well established. They exist under the control of drug cartels involved in the cocaine business. These drug cartels rule the favela with an iron fist, dealing out their own punishments to anyone who breaks the cartel's rules. For example, if a person informs the police about drug cartel activity, they are killed. Some people living in the favela work for the drug cartels, as they make quick and easy money. However, many other people in the favela work in low-paying honest jobs, struggling to get by. The police are supposed to protect the inhabitants in addition to stopping the flow of drugs from the cartels. Policing in the favela is not like in Australia. The police in Rio de Janeiro are very poorly paid, and some are involved in corruption and bribery.

Paulo was a one such policeman working in the favela district of Rio. He was in charge of a squad of eight policemen who were responsible for patrolling an area in one of the worst favelas in the city. Paulo was also an occupational psychopath. He abused the authority of his position in every conceivable way, and showed no remorse for his behaviour at all. In fact, Paulo went beyond the corruption typical of police in Rio, he took the meaning of the word exploitation to an entirely new level. He would sell confiscated drugs back to the drug dealers, he would 'arrest' young girls and sexually assault them, he would demand payments from very poor families for protection, and one of his favourite activities was to go down into the city area of Rio and 'fine' tourists, insisting they pay their fine in cash on the spot. In short, Paulo was a corrupt policeman who used his job to serve his own needs. He also bullied his squad so that they became passive participants in the corruption by not reporting anything to their superiors. In the end Paulo and all of his squad were fired from the police.

It is clear from his actions that Paulo shows behaviours typical of each of the three psychopath sub-types. He bullied and manipulated his co-workers for his own gain (organisational psychopath), he stole items seized during his work and fraudulently sold them again (corporate criminal psychopath), and he sexually assaulted as well as committing other violent crimes (violent criminal psychopath). However, Paulo is fundamentally different from the other sub-types of workplace psychopath. He did not want to climb the ranks in the police force (organisational psychopath), nor did he want to make money fraudulently (corporate criminal psychopath) or only commit violent crime (violent criminal psychopath). What is unique about

Paulo, and indeed the occupational psychopath, is that they use their job to conceal their psychopathic behaviours. Paulo enjoyed the power and control over other people that his job allowed him. The money and other items he stole were simply an additional benefit.

The occupational psychopath is unique because they are able to use their job to enact their psychopathic tendencies on people external to the job itself, and this is not done solely to physically destroy or for financial gain. However, they are also similar to the other workplace psychopath sub-types because they do not have a conscience, and therefore feel no remorse or guilt for any of their behaviours. Everything they do is in their own self-interest. How they satisfy these needs is what sets them apart from other workplace psychopaths.

8

WORKPLACE PSYCHOPATHS – ARE THEY GOOD FOR BUSINESS?

CAN A WORKPLACE PSYCHOPATH be of benefit to the company they work for? Is it possible for a person with no conscience or remorse to use their personality characteristics to make more money for themselves and/or their employer? At what human cost does this profit come?

The answers to these questions are complex. Each answer depends on a number of factors including what industry the psychopath is working in, what sub-type of workplace psychopath is being referred to, and who is evaluating the value of the psychopath. A shareholder will provide a different answer to a CEO, who will provide a different answer again to a customer or the person who has to work with the workplace psychopath.

The simple answer to whether a psychopath can be useful to a company is no. In the short term they can generate sales with their verbal abilities, or persuade people in the company to take new directions, but in the long term the company will usually suffer. This is because the psychopath, regardless of sub-type or profession, is concerned with only one thing – self-gratification. This self-gratification is obtained irrespective of the cost to people around them, or to the company they work for. Unless the psychopath's self-interest is the same as that of the company, the company will ultimately lose. Moreover, even if the psychopath and the company share similar goals, the psychopath often alienates and exploits co-workers to achieve this goal. This can result in the loss of valued, highly trained staff which ultimately comes out of the company bottom-line.

The financial cost does not even begin to account for the psychological damage caused to co-workers.

What is 'good for business'?

Corporations generally measure their success in terms of how much money they make, while government agencies critique how effectively they perform their legislated responsibilities. Employees are viewed as a means to an end, resources used to make money or enforce legislation.

Therefore 'good for business' would be defined by the decision makers in big business and government as the amount of profit made each year, or the number of times and effectiveness with which legislation is enforced. Secondary considerations include employee welfare, staff retention rates, sick leave taken by each employee, training costs, and human resources and recruitment costs. Each of these secondary considerations is emphasised because they can affect the productivity of staff, and therefore the amount of profit made or quality of services delivered.

In recent years, corporations began to realise that the better they treated their employees, the more productivity they observed for each worker. This philosophy is still reflected in the development of numerous workplace programs designed to make employees feel a part of the 'corporate culture', to reduce stress in the workplace, to emphasise that they are valued employees, etc. It is important to note that the success of these programs is measured in terms of increases in productivity or decreases in costs such as sick leave and employee resignations.

Society's view of what is 'good for business' does not necessarily take into account employee welfare unless this issue is affecting profits. This approach is not motivated by sinister forces that control and exploit workers for the sake of a few wealthy people in society. It is simply a product of living in a capitalist economy whereby society revolves around the exchange of goods and services for money. The vast majority of businesses are started with the aim of making money. Large businesses are usually accountable to shareholders, who are only concerned with how much profit the company makes each year as this affects how much money they will receive as a dividend, as well as the value of their stocks. The directors of the company are employed on the understanding that they will endeavour to make the largest possible profit each year for the company. Therefore employees are seen as a resource needed to provide goods and services that can be exchanged for money. If the employees function well together, the company makes more money. From this perspective, the workplace psychopath is evaluated in terms of how much additional income they can contribute to the company.

From a government agency perspective, the psychopath is evaluated in terms of how well they achieve the agency goals, whatever these may be. Government agencies generally focus on productivity, employee welfare is covered under the award agreements, but it is not necessarily a priority to provide working conditions that exceed those defined by the award.

I would argue that as a society, it is also important to measure success in both business and government agencies in terms of balancing the human cost with profitability and service provision. Unfortunately, it is often the case that providing better working conditions for employees impacts on profitability or service provision, and therefore the human cost becomes a secondary issue.

This chapter will evaluate whether each sub-type of psychopath is good for business from both a profitability/service provision perspective in addition to looking at the human cost of employing a psychopath.

How beneficial is each sub-type of workplace psychopath?

The organisational psychopath

At first glance, the organisational psychopath may appear to have significant contributions they can make to a company. They possess good verbal skills, are experienced at manipulating people, are prepared to do whatever it takes to achieve their goals, and they may be creative as a result of their being prone to boredom leading to the development of new ideas. In the short term, these attributes may lead to increased revenue. However, this positive contribution can be misleading.

A relatively new concept in the business world is Customer Relationship Management (CRM). This philosophy became popular in the 1990s, and in essence it states that a critical business principle is to ensure a good relationship exists between the business and desirable customers. This promotes repeat business, which is valuable because marketing the company services is no longer necessary as the customer is already familiar with the product or service. Put simply, managing the relationship between your company and the customer is important so that they continue to purchase goods or services from your company.

In the short term, the organisational psychopath may generate sales, or embark on ambitious projects that promise to make the firm large sums of money. The customer is happy as they have been promised big things and the company is happy as they look forward to receiving additional income. However, as we have already seen, the organisational psychopath will not hesitate to lie about what they can deliver. In addition, they are not prepared to actually do the work required, making up excuses for why it is not completed and blaming everyone other than themselves. This causes the customer to become very dissatisfied in the long term, and they cancel the contract. From a CRM perspective, the customer will not be returning to do business with the company again. Worse, they tell other companies about their bad experience with the psychopath and the company they work for, creating negativity and uncertainty about the company who did not deliver as promised. This company then has to advertise not only their product, but they also have to convince people that they are reliable and can deliver goods or services as promised. The value of this damage caused by the psychopath cannot be calculated. What is the cost to a company of losing their reputation. In some cases it can be bankruptcy.

So in the short term the organisational psychopath may generate additional profit, but in the long term the company loses as their reputation has been damaged, sometimes beyond repair. From a profit perspective, the organisational psychopath is not desirable.

The human cost of employing an organisational psychopath in a company can be astronomical, both financially for the company and psychologically for the victims. The financial cost to the company often easily exceeds the profit the psychopath makes for the company in the initial stages of their employment. Staff resigning, recruitment costs, training costs for new staff, and legal actions taken against the company all add up to substantial amounts of money. Authors Helene Richards and Sheila Freeman in *Bullying in the Workplace: An Occupational Hazard* estimate that in Australia $36 billion is lost due to damages payouts to former employees and loss of productivity as a result of bullying. Perhaps more importantly, organisational psychopaths take away from time that the company could be using to generate additional business or expand relationships held with current customers.

From a legislative perspective, each company has a duty of care to their employees to ensure that no personal harm is caused to them as a result of their work. In theory this precludes an organisational psychopath being employed in many cases. In practice, companies do not deliberately employ the organisational psychopath. Therefore the question must be asked, should companies be doing more to detect organisational psychopaths entering their organisation, and should they implement policies that increase the probability of such psychopaths being detected and managed once they are working in an organisation. One final, but very important question concerns the rights of the organisational psychopath themselves. How does one achieve a balance between the rights of the psychopath and the rights of their victims not to be victimised? Is it discrimination to sack an employee solely on the grounds of having a personality disorder such as psychopathy? All of these questions must be answered before a solution to the issue of psychopaths in the workplace can be resolved.

The corporate criminal psychopath

The corporate criminal psychopath has very few benefits for any organisation that employs them. One of the few benefits they may provide for the company is that they often work hard on their 'legitimate' work to cover their fraudulent activity. However, the cost to the company in the long run exceeds the value this sub-type of psychopath adds to the company. Furthermore, the corporate criminal psychopath may be involved in more than simply defrauding their company, posing a real risk to fellow co-workers. The financial and human cost of employing this type of psychopath exceeds any benefits.

The violent criminal psychopath

The violent criminal psychopath has no benefits for a conventional business in terms of financial contributions and human costs. In fact, it is not uncommon for them to sabotage their own and other people's work equipment so that they are given time off as they cannot complete their duties.

However, the violent criminal psychopath can have significant benefits when 'employed' by law enforcement agencies as informants. The difficulty lies in identifying what is valuable information and what is untrue or outdated information that is of no use, as the world of informants is very murky indeed.

The key to evaluating the value of information provided by an informant is based on the principle that the violent criminal psychopath is self-serving at all times. If there is a benefit to them providing the information to law enforcement, it is most probably useful information. For example, it is not uncommon for drug dealers to provide information to police about a rival drug dealer. The police make an arrest, and the drug dealer has less competition, thereby increasing their 'market share'.

Again it is evident that the violent criminal psychopath is of benefit only when it serves their own interests. Unfortunately the motives underlying their original offer of information is not always clear. Therefore the decision made by law enforcement to employ them as an informant is a complicated one.

The occupational psychopath

The occupational psychopath has no positive financial, service provision, or human cost benefits. They perform their jobs adequately enough to evade detection as an occupational psychopath, but do not contribute anything above what is required. By definition they use their jobs to identify and recruit victims, and this has no benefits for anyone apart from themselves. Therefore they can only have a negative impact on any organisation they work for. Moreover, they have a decidedly negative impact on the members of the public they encounter through their place of work or profession.

Position vacant – psychopath wanted

I am often asked at the end of lectures I give on workplace psychopaths whether there are any jobs that are particularly suited to a person with psychopathy.

People often suggest that a psychopath may be a good special forces soldier; auditor; spy; loss prevention officer; salesman; security guard; and prison officer. It is common to assume the psychopath would do well in high risk or exciting professions.

Intuitively it makes sense to suggest that a person with no conscience, who is prone to boredom and constantly needs excitement would make a good special forces soldier for example. However, when one examines all of the personality characteristics of the psychopath, it becomes readily apparent that they are not desirable employees for any of the above positions.

Special forces soldier – A special forces soldier requires strong discipline and motivation to perform a task that may test the limits of human endurance. They also require the ability to follow orders, be responsible, and not act impulsively as their colleagues may be injured or even killed if they make a mistake. The psychopath possesses none of these qualities. The fact that they would not feel bad about killing another person as part of their job is not sufficient to make them a good soldier. In *Without Conscience*, Dr Robert Hare describes a study done by one of his students, David Cox, examining whether psychopaths would make good bomb disposal experts as they are 'cool under fire' and have a strong need for excitement. David Cox found that the bomb disposal experts referred to psychopaths as 'dangerous cowboys', unreliable and impulsive individuals who lacked the perfectionism and attention to detail needed to stay alive. Dr Hare adds that it is just as unlikely that psychopaths would make good spies, as they are impulsive, are concerned only for the moment, and do not have any allegiance to people or causes. This makes them 'unpredictable, careless, and undependable – likely to be "loose cannons"' (p. 62).

Salesperson – The psychopath is likely to be a very good salesperson, if they are intelligent as well as glib and superficial. In fact, a study done in 2001 by Marc Hamer found that superior sales performance was associated with higher levels of narcissism (egocentric and grandiose), sociopathy, and cognitive empathy. This suggests that some psychopathic characteristics may contribute to successful sales abilities. Cognitive empathy refers to an understanding of how the client is thinking, allowing the salesperson to tailor a sales strategy to a particular individual. Interestingly, Hamer found that emotional empathy was not associated with superior sales performance. In other words, the ability to empathise with the way other people are feeling emotionally did not affect sales performance. The psychopath does not have the ability to emotionally empathise with other people.

Unfortunately, the psychopath as a salesperson is only of benefit in the short term as has been previously mentioned. In the long term they let clients down. In addition, the psychopath who is a salesperson is likely to exploit the system in some way to benefit themselves. For example they may steal products or sell them at 'discount rates' to their friends.

The psychopath as salesperson is one situation in which a management strategy can be an effective way of controlling the psychopath's behaviour at the same time as using their excellent sales skills. If the psychopath wants to make money and have little supervision, and the company goal is to make money, these two goals can be aligned with certain guidelines implemented. These guidelines may include the psychopath paying for any lost or 'stolen' items from their commission, the psychopath is not authorised to sell anything apart from their line of products, and the psychopath must agree to the company randomly contacting and 'debriefing' some of his or her clients to verify legitimate sales techniques are being used.

Loss prevention/auditor – People often assume that if a psychopath can break rules and escape detection, they must have a superior set of skills they can use to spot other psychopaths who are also breaking the rules. This assumption is plausible, but it ignores the self-serving nature of the psychopath. It is highly likely that the psychopath can make more money as an auditor or loss prevention person who steals goods or money than they can from an honest wage. It is also possible that the psychopath could team up with the person they are supposed to be identifying as a thief or fraudster, and implement an undetectable system for stealing from their employer. These positions also place a certain amount of trust in the psychopath with inadequate monitoring procedures in place. After all, who audits the auditors?

However, a management system can also be implemented to ensure they do their detection job properly. For example, if a bonus is given for every theft identified by the psychopath, they may be able to earn more money than if they stole the goods. In addition, the psychopath may enjoy the excitement of chasing another dishonest person.

Security officer/prison guard – Just because a person is a psychopath does not mean they have a greater understanding of how other psychopaths think. Security officers and prison guards are suggested as ideal occupations for the psychopath as they detect crime in the case of the security guard; and they have power over other people in the case of the prison guard. A number of case studies have been illustrated in previous chapters identifying why it is dangerous to allow a psychopath to be a security guard, they abuse the trust that goes with the position. The psychopath would not make a good prison guard because they would be likely to abuse their authority over the people they were responsible for. The only reason a psychopath would apply to be a prison guard is because they were an occupational psychopath who saw the inmates as easy to access victims. They would be ineffective in terms of rehabilitation and correcting criminal behaviours, as it would not interest them at all.

Psychopathic corporations – do they exist?
One interesting area concerns the similarity between corporate 'values' and psychopathy. Can the tactics

and strategies used by organisations to achieve their goals be called psychopathic? If one goes through some of the psychopathy characteristics, a number of aspects of corporate behaviour may be considered 'psychopathic'.

However, given that a corporation is not one individual, corporations clearly cannot be diagnosed as psychopaths. The criteria are discussed to promote awareness of how a corporate culture may reflect certain values that are synonymous with psychopathy. Corporations in Western society are largely driven by competition, and the question needs to be asked: 'At what point does a win at all costs attitude and competitive behaviour resemble psychopathy?'

The characteristics listed below are intriguing to think about.

- *Glib and superficial* – A number of organisations hire public relations and media consultants to create a certain image surrounding their company by using 'catchy' expressions and rather superficial terminology. For example, the majority of advertisements could be considered glib and superficial, showing customers all the positive aspects of a good or service and glossing over any bad aspects.

- *Egocentric and grandiose* – Many organisations are self-focused and filled with a sense that they need to continue to grow and become 'market leaders' or the most important corporation in their market.

- *Lack of remorse or guilt* – Corporations 'feel' the exact opposite of remorse or guilt when a competitor collapses or 'dies' as a result of their actions.

The corporation views this as one less competitor in the marketplace that will result in them achieving greater market share. The 'death' of another corporation is seen as an opportunity. Some corporations actively seek the economic collapse of competitors, doing everything they can to 'kill' their competitors financially.

- *Deceitful and manipulative* – Corporations are not always honest. In fact, in some large corporations that have recently been investigated by government regulators, a culture of deception and manipulation of shareholders and customers appeared to be the 'norm'. It would be interesting to know how many other companies deceive shareholders and clients in the interest of 'making a profit'.

- *Parasitic* – It could be construed as parasitic or living off other people's unfortunate circumstance when large multinationals 'exploit' poorly paid workers in third world countries. Many multinationals have factories in third world nations where their products are made at minimum cost (because they exploit very poor workers) and then sell these goods at significant profit levels in the Western world. Public opinion has made this practice less appealing from a public relations point of view. Some multinationals stopped using third world factories, and bought the same items from the same third world factories through sub-contractors so that the multinational could deny exploiting third world workers. This could be seen as manipulative and deceptive behaviour motivated by profit (or the 'self-gratification' of the company).

A paradox seems to exist between individual human versus corporate goals when it comes to co-existence and altruistic behaviour. Corporations are encouraged to compete with each other and win at all costs. In contrast, individuals are encouraged to work together in social networks, otherwise society would not function effectively. Corporations are encouraged to be driven by self-interest, individuals are encouraged to think about what is good for the society and put their own self-interests second to societal goals. Social cohesiveness is crucial to the survival of the human race.

Would it be possible for the human race to survive if every person on earth had the same values and attitudes as corporations do toward other corporations and customers?

9

THE HUMAN COST OF WORKPLACE PSYCHOPATHS

FOR THREE YEARS Jason had worked for a boss who made his working life unbearable. He was faced with unrealistic deadlines for his work projects, his boss would blame him for work not done, would shout and humiliate him in front of his co-workers, encourage other colleagues to ignore or criticise Jason, and generally make Jason feel totally inadequate and rattle his self-esteem. His boss displayed all the behaviours associated with an organisational psychopath.

Jason became increasingly anxious, not only about his job, but about his life. When he first joined the agency he worked for, he noticed that his boss was bullying him in subtle ways, and he was shocked, as he had never experienced this sort of behaviour. Jason realised what was happening to him and felt angry. As a result, Jason's work life began taking up more of his non-working time.

When Jason tried to confide in his friends about

what was happening, some told him that he just had to live with the situation, others implied or said he was exaggerating the situation. He felt betrayed because people did not understand what was happening. Other friends and family members were pushed away because Jason felt increasingly isolated from the people around him. He also felt ashamed because he believed he had allowed himself to be bullied.

While Jason was slowly withdrawing from people, he was developing a hatred for his boss. He would often think about ways to 'get back' at him, and he even thought about killing him at one stage when the psychological pain became unbearable. Jason would frequently shout at his boss at work, accusing him of being incompetent and a bully. In response his boss would insist that Jason receive 'disciplinary counselling' and these outbursts were recorded on his personnel file. Jason's boss was making sure that Jason's reputation and career were being systematically ruined.

The frequent 'disciplinary counselling' sessions, combined with the massive amount of work Jason was delegated made him feel completely overwhelmed about everything in his life. He began to question his professional capability, his intelligence, and even his ability to relate to other people. He thought it might have been his fault that all of this was happening to him.

Jason also began to experience panic attacks, which made him feel as though he was about to die. He did not know what to do, or who to turn to as it seemed like everything he did led to more psychological pain and suffering. He realised his boss was the problem and believed that any problem could be solved if you were prepared to put in enough time and effort. Jason was convinced that he could 'fix' the situation. As the situation got worse, Jason felt guilty about not being able to solve such a 'simple' problem.

Jason didn't know what to do. The overwhelming problem at work was taking a toll on his personal life – he suffered a relationship break-up, he felt more and more powerless and out of control, he had trouble sleeping (lack of sleep made it harder for him to cope), and depression set in. Thoughts of suicide began to consume Jason. Life was no longer positive for him.

Jason complained to those higher up in the agency but his concerns were ignored and he was made to feel like he was the undesirable employee. By chance, Jason read an article on workplace psychopaths and decided to get professional help. He came to understand what he was up against and knew that continuing to fight would be futile – no job was worth the psychological trauma he was suffering. Jason made the brave decision to leave and regain his life and self-esteem.

When faced with a workplace psychopath's destructive behaviour, regardless of which sub-type, victims characteristically report feeling as though they have lost control over their lives. Panic attacks, depression, disturbed sleep and nightmares, relationship problems, confusion, disbelief, guilt, lack of trust, anger, powerlessness, flashbacks, shame, embarrassment and sexual dysfunction are just a few examples of how these victims suffer.

Some longer-term effects also include being unable to look for another job, as they do not trust people or themselves any more, or a loss of confidence in the ability to perform adequately in their chosen profession or career.

Employees who choose to stay in the workplace, despite the trauma, frequently report feeling resentment toward the company they have given so much to; they believe it has let them down by not believing or protecting them.

Victim selection – why me?

Perhaps the most common of all questions asked by victims is 'Why me?'. There is no specific personality trait that psychopaths look for when targeting their victims. Any number of factors can influence how they select a victim including random chance, the way a victim looks, the way a victim talks, victim intelligence, victim profession, how altruistic the victim is, and even what other people think of the victim.

A psychopath is more likely to inflict greater psychological and/or financial damage on a person who is lonely or has low self-esteem. This is because the psychopath is able to push a vulnerable person's buttons more easily rather than someone who is confident about themselves and their abilities. People who have few or no friends are also easy targets, as they have no social support network to rely on when they are faced with the workplace psychopath's relentless campaign.

Joseph had never felt intelligent or confident. He was always trying to prove that he was more capable than anyone else at work. As a university student he was always studying, aiming for top marks in every subject.

Lisa, Joseph's manager, was an organisational psychopath. She was able to use Joseph's insecurity to manipulate him into doing the tasks that were assigned to her. She would take credit for his work. Joseph focused on Lisa's praise, and measured himself as a valuable person because of the many jobs Lisa gave him to do. He also believed that Lisa was romantically interested in him, which was deliberately used by her to keep Joseph loyal and under control. Joseph would spy on Lisa's staff (his colleagues) and report back to her about anything that could make her look bad to her supervisors. When Lisa was promoted, Joseph was forgotten, as he was no longer useful. This rejection confirmed everything he believed about himself; that he was a stupid person who no one had any reason to like. His self-esteem plummeted.

Four years after this experience Joseph is still too scared to expose himself emotionally to anyone either at work or in a relationship. He does not trust anyone enough to risk being hurt again. Rationally he believes that Lisa used him, but emotionally this is still too painful for him to deal with.

Once the workplace psychopath has identified a victim, they use the strategies identified in previous chapters to 'hook' their victim. These strategies involve playing on the victim's greed (corporate criminal psychopath), inducing fear (occupational and violent criminal psychopaths), and manipulating people and company rules around them so that their victim becomes increasingly helpless (organisational psychopath).

Whatever strategy the workplace psychopath uses against the victim, a number of similar responses are observed.

What's happening to me?

Many people who have been physically, financially, psychologically, or sexually victimised by a workplace psychopath of any sub-type have described experiencing a range of reactions and feelings from shock and disbelief, to anger and anxiety. While we all experience these sorts of feelings in the workplace at some stage in our working lives, it is the prolonged manipulation by a workplace psychopath to create these reactions that has a damaging effect. By learning to deal with these reactions in a positive way, the victim has a greater chance of surviving an encounter with a psychopath.

Shock and disbelief

When a person realises that they are being or have been manipulated or directly confronted by a psychopath, they can experience a sense of shock and disbelief, that 'it cannot be happening'. Some victims also say that they find it hard to accept that the confrontation or manipulation has happened, and feel that it must be them going crazy or imagining things, or blowing the situation out of proportion.

Mary's area manager tried to sexually assault her while they were at a conference. He forced his way in to her room after a night of drinking and tried to kiss her. When Mary refused, he slapped her across the face and forced her to lie on the bed. Mary screamed and he ran from the room. Mary lay on her bed in absolute shock and terror that he would return. She then began to question whether it had really happened at all; it felt as though she was imagining the entire thing. When she went in to the bathroom and saw the red marks on her face, she knew it was real. However, Mary did not report the area manager as he had a family and she did not want to break it up. She rationalised that he was drunk, and really was not such a bad person; maybe she was exaggerating what happened in her own mind. Mary's area manager was later fired for sexually harassing a different victim.

Anger

Victims of workplace psychopaths may feel anger and hatred towards the psychopath for many different reasons. Anger is an emotion that people generally direct at others when they believe something bad or unfair is happening. This emotion usually goes hand-in-hand with a feeling of being threatened or unsafe. Sometimes this anger is not directed at the psychopath but towards someone close to the victim. This displaced anger happens when the victim cannot react or finds it difficult to get angry at the workplace psychopath.

Angry reactions can include impatience, acting on impulse, saying things that are regretted later, or becoming physically or verbally aggressive. Frequent anger reactions can become physically and emotionally draining, affect concentration and interfere with people's happiness and relationships. Long-term anger can affect the body's immune system, cause high blood pressure, increase the risk of heart disease and hypertension. It can also lead to alcohol or drug abuse as a form of self-medication to alleviate suffering being felt.

Feeling angry can often interfere with a person's ability to think rationally and clearly about the situation. The victim focuses on perceived violations and the injustices done to them by the psychopath, which can increase the feelings of anger. Victims often cannot stop thinking about the situation. Victims report mentally rehearsing every single detail of their exchange with the workplace psychopath, speculating about what may have happened 'if only' they had said or done something differently.

Another strategy is for the victim to become passive-aggressive. Passive-aggression is when a person tries to punish or hurt another person by using subtle strategies such as silence or withdrawing of attention. They may ignore or respond coldly to the psychopath and promise to do work they have no intention of completing. This sort of strategy generally exacerbates the situation for the victim.

Fear and anxiety

A feeling of apprehension and dread that something bad is going to happen is another response felt by a psychopath victim. Characteristically these people fear other people, being in the presence of the psychopath, and the physical environment of their workplace.

Anxiety, like anger, is a state of physiological arousal that is often accompanied by unpleasant symptoms such as shortness of breath, sweaty palms, dry mouth, pounding heartbeat, muscle tension and tightness in the chest. Everyone feels anxious occasionally, it is a useful survival mechanism. However, continual feelings of anxiety that come from the person believing they can't escape the psychopath in their workplace becomes chronic anxiety. This is one of the most crippling psychological conditions as it stifles people's ability to enjoy life because they are always anxious and stressed.

The workplace psychopath poses a threat to all areas of the victim's life. They are a danger to physical safety, as all sub-types of workplace psychopath have been known to use physical violence. They threaten material wellbeing as they commonly cause people to leave their jobs, causing the victim to make a lifestyle change or even face financial ruin. Self-esteem is also threatened as the workplace psychopath aims to control and dominate another person by destroying their victim's self-esteem. Finally, the workplace psychopath is a major threat to their victim's social safety because they encourage people around the victim to disapprove of them in some way. The workplace psychopath also publicly degrades and humiliates the victim, further reducing their confidence in their own social position.

Feeling anxious is not only a physical sensation. Anxiety also influences how victims think about their situation at work and at home. Feeling anxious can cause 'tunnel vision' that focuses victim attention on whatever is making them feel anxious. Tunnel vision limits the victim's ability to think clearly or to process other information in a normal way. For example, if a person is anxious about the behaviour of a workplace psychopath, they may plan to talk with the psychopath but then become so nervous that they cannot remember what they wanted to say. The person feels more helpless and their self-esteem plummets even lower.

Signs of stress

While not all stress in the workplace is caused by the workplace psychopath, some signs of workplace stress include:

- Feeling irritable.
- Having trouble concentrating.
- Tiredness.
- Loss of sense of humour.
- Increasing number of arguments with people around you.
- Lower productivity at work.
- Sick more often.
- Lack of concern about your work.
- Attending work each day becomes an effort.
- Loss of interest in activities outside of work.

Shame and embarrassment

Some victims feel ashamed or embarrassed that they can't deal with a workplace psychopath. They also describe feeling as though everyone around them is aware of what is happening to them, and these people judge them as weak and useless. They often interpret what people say to them as relating to their specific experience and react inappropriately.

Feelings of shame and embarrassment can become so overwhelming that they impair a person's ability to function. Some victims refuse to interact with other people as they fear their 'secret' will be discovered.

Fear of not being believed

Because psychopaths in the workplace are not recognised as a widespread problem, victims often report a fear that no one will believe the terrible things that have been done to them. Often this fear of not being believed is reinforced when a manager or colleague does not believe the victim's allegations against the workplace psychopath. Fear of not being believed increases the sense of isolation, making them more vulnerable to the strategies used by the psychopath.

Sue had been living with a man who beat her repeatedly. He would treat her extremely badly, but he never left marks on her that could not be covered up by Sue's clothing. Sue kept her bruises covered because she was ashamed she 'let' the abuse happen. Everyone thought Sue's husband was fantastic; he was extremely charming in public and social situations. The neighbours thought he was great, Sue's family felt very fortunate that Sue had met such a nice man, and her husband's work colleagues enjoyed working with him.

When Sue finally reported what had been happening to the police, all of her 'friends' told her not to be foolish and make up things about her husband. That was until Sue showed them her bruises. It also turned out that Sue's husband had been embezzling money from his firm to cover gambling debts and expenses incurred from having a mistress who lived in a luxurious apartment and enjoyed first-class international travel. Some of her husband's colleagues still cannot believe it. They assumed a corporate and violent criminal psychopath would appear 'abnormal', not someone who was a trusted friend and colleague for many years.

Guilt and confusion

People often feel guilt about their inability to stand up to the workplace psychopath. They blame themselves for being manipulated or attacked. This self-blame and guilt can lead to confusion about the best course of action as the victim becomes caught up with anxiety trying to solve what seems like an unsolvable problem.

Feeling powerless, out of control or 'going crazy'

Victims of a workplace psychopath often feel there is a lack of control in their life. They find that their thoughts and behaviours are dominated by the workplace psychopath; constantly thinking about work and what they could have or should have done in certain situations. They have no control over when or how the psychopath is going to mistreat them. These people feel powerless and unable to change their situation.

The victim's interactions with other people often change as a result. This reinforces the feeling of being out of control because everything in their life appears to be changing, and it is negative or detrimental change. Life feels different for them. Once the victim thinks their life has changed, they often feel power-lessness because they cannot see any way of going back to their old life and feeling happy.

Lack of trust and a fear of people

The lack of trust of others is a direct result of the psychopath's continuous manipulation of the victim. The victim loses faith in other human beings as they have learned that people cause them emotional and sometimes physical pain. The fact that many victims initially liked and believed the psychopath when they first encountered them contributes to a loss of confidence in their ability to identify people who may be physically or psychologically dangerous.

Leanne was victimised so badly by an organisational psychopath that she was forced to leave a job that she initially loved. She attended numerous counselling sessions in which she developed strategies to find work and rebuild her self-esteem. Leanne eventually found a new job. The people she worked with were nice, but Leanne did not trust them. She openly documented everything they said and did in case she needed to use any of the information in future legal action. Her colleagues felt intimidated by this behaviour and did not interact with her. Leanne felt socially isolated and eventually quit her job. She believed that she was right not to trust anybody, as she did not actually get hurt when she was isolated by her colleagues. She had no insight that if she had opened herself up to them, she probably would have stayed in the job and regained some of her trust in other people.

Flashbacks

Victims often find that they keep replaying incidents where they were victimised by the psychopath. After a while, these constant thoughts may become flashbacks which are triggered by things that remind them of the incidents. For example, a particular smell, time of day, specific locations, or seeing someone who resembles the workplace psychopath.

Sleep disturbances and nightmares

Disrupted sleeping patterns are another result of victimisation. This can include an inability to get to sleep (insomnia), or oversleeping (hypersomnia). Nightmares can also be a common response although this usually settles down after some time has passed since the last incident experienced by the victim.

Relationship problems

Loss of trust in other people, a desire to be alone, a desire to be with someone all the time, and difficulties in intimate relationships are other outcomes from workplace victimisation. Because of the extreme effect on the victim, the workplace psychopath also has a negative impact on the victim's families and friends.

Depression

Everyone feels upset or sad from time to time, often triggered by disappointment or loss. Depression is a debilitating condition that interferes with a person's ability to experience pleasure, interact with other people, and participate in life. There are various degrees of sadness and depression, including a depressed mood, dysthymic disorder, and major or clinical depression.

Depressed mood is an emotional state that makes people feel sad, miserable, low and flat. Generally it passes after a short period of time. When a workplace psychopath is involved in causing depressed mood, this can become chronic and the depressed mood can last for long periods of time.

Dysthymic disorder is chronic mild depression. Victims feel constantly sad, pessimistic or generally apathetic. Other symptoms include low energy, low self-esteem, irritability, guilt, poor concentration, and difficulty making decisions.

Major depression is a more severe and disabling condition than dysthymic disorder. It includes low energy, loss of interest in things and a lack of pleasure. Major depression can be mild, moderate or severe. People with mild depression are still able to function, though they experience little joy in doing so. People with moderate depression have greater social and occupational impairment. They may achieve little because of poor concentration or inability to relate to other people. People with severe depression experience a range of symptoms including changes in appetite, lack of energy, recurrent thoughts of death to name a few, and their ability to do anything at all is extremely limited. Even minor tasks such as getting out of bed or getting breakfast seem challenging to them.

To be diagnosed with depression, five of the following characteristics (including at least one of the first two symptoms) should be experienced for at least a two-week period:

- Depressed mood for much of the day.
- Reduced interest in pleasurable activities.
- Changes in appetite or weight.
- Changes in sleep patterns.
- Lack of energy.
- Feelings of guilt or worthlessness.
- Agitation or slowing down of physical movements.
- Inability to concentrate or make decisions.
- Recurrent thoughts of death or suicide.

Getting help

If you or someone you know is experiencing one or a number of these symptoms, it is important that professional assistance is sought. A number of different types of professionals can help in these types of situation. A psychiatrist, psychologist or counsellor can all help in different ways. It is important that the professional is well trained and experienced in dealing with issues that arise from contact with a workplace psychopath or other types of dysfunctional workplace behaviours.

Before getting help, it is useful for a victim to note what symptoms they are experiencing as a result of the workplace psychopath's treatment, such as:

- Anxiety, stress, excessive worry about your situation at work.
- Inability to sleep.
- Racing heart.
- Hyperventilation (fast, shallow breathing).
- Inability to concentrate.
- Tension headaches or migraines.
- Shame or embarrassment that result in a noticeable personality change.
- Butterflies in the stomach while on the way to, going home from, or at work.
- Aching or tired joints and muscles.
- Depression.
- Any skin complaints such as rashes, shingles, etc, that occur after the harassment started.
- Abuse or overuse of substances such as alcohol, tobacco, prescription or illegal drugs to cope with the situation.
- Hair loss.
- High blood pressure.
- Stomach ulcers.
- Suicidal thoughts (*you should see someone immediately if you are experiencing this*).
- Chronic Fatigue Syndrome.
- Glandular fever.
- Significant weight loss or gain.
- A feeling of exhaustion.
- Feeling irritable or on edge all the time.

- Difficulty trusting or believing in anybody.
- Relationship problems (more fights, etc).
- Loss of interest in sexual activity.

It is also important for victims of the workplace psychopath not to feel as though they are experiencing the stress alone. Family and friends should be involved in the process if the victim feels comfortable with this, as they can provide very important support networks at a difficult time in the victim's life.

10
PROTECTING YOURSELF

MANAGING AND CURING the workplace psychopath
are two very different propositions. Curing the workplace psychopath involves permanently changing their
personality and behaviours; managing the workplace
psychopath involves controlling their behaviours to
minimise risk of harm to fellow co-workers.

Managing the workplace psychopath
Managing the psychopath in any workplace is always
a complex balancing act between the rights of the
psychopath, other company employees, clients and
the organisation itself. The ethical responsibilities when
dealing with a workplace psychopath are also significant factors. For example, most co-workers who are
being victimised want the organisation to fire the psychopath. However, this may violate the rights of the
psychopath if it is plausible to manage their behaviour.

Psychopath management strategies are based on the characteristics of the individual psychopath, as well as who the psychopath is victimising. Victims can include superiors, colleagues at the same level, people junior to the psychopath, and/or people external to the organisation. In some cases, not all of the victims are in positions that allow them to manage the workplace psychopath.

Can all sub-types of workplace psychopath be managed?

The simple answer to this question is no. Three of the four sub-types of workplace psychopath primarily exploit or harm their victims in criminal or under-handed ways that cannot be 'managed' by the organisation they work for. In reality, it is only the organisational psychopath that can be managed. With the other three sub-types of psychopaths, all that corporations or government agencies can do is deal with the consequences of employing the psychopath by implementing strategies to look after remaining workers and other traumatised victims. Profiling these workplace psychopath sub-types is a more effective preventative strategy that minimises damage by identifying them early in their careers.

The corporate criminal psychopath defrauds people and/or organisations. If fraudulent behaviour was identified by an organisation, the most appropriate action would be to report the criminal activity to the relevant law enforcement authorities. Generally the corporate criminal psychopath does not come to notice for their fraudulent activities until after they are caught, therefore the organisation is not aware that they need to manage this sub-type of psychopath until it is too late.

The violent criminal psychopath cannot be managed by the organisation that employs them for similar reasons. If an organisation was aware that an employee was performing violent criminal behaviours they would be obliged to report this to the police. Organisations cannot and should not attempt to manage the behaviour of these sub-types.

The occupational psychopath is usually not identified until after they have harmed their victims. Once the occupational psychopath is identified, it becomes clear that they have breached internal policies or guidelines, and it is often mandatory to discipline or fire them.

How to manage the organisational workplace psychopath

There are a number of general principles that apply to managing the organisational psychopath. Perhaps the most important management principles come from research done by psychologists in human learning, organisational psychology, forensic psychology and clinical psychology.

There are a number of overall aims in any organisational psychopath management plan:

1. To ensure all employees have a safe working environment, free from threat of physical and/or psychological harm.
2. To reduce staff resignation rates by eliminating 'antisocial' behaviour within the organisation.

3. To promote an organisational reputation as a favoured employer, encouraging promising and skilled employees to work in the organisation, thereby increasing profitability.
4. To increase productivity by reducing or eliminating the negative effects of the organisational psychopath on other employees' work output.
5. To minimise or eliminate damage caused to the organisation's reputation as a result of unethical, manipulative or deceptive organisational psychopath work practices.

The management plan itself must be a collaborative effort between organisation members and a consultant who is an expert in the area of organisational psychopaths and dysfunctional workplace behaviours.

An organisational psychopath management strategy generally includes a number of components. First, an assessment of the organisation is carried out. Costs and benefits of employing the psychopath are measured. Simultaneously, a review of existing policies the organisation has in place to deal with the psychopathic employee is undertaken. Also, the individual who has been nominated by the organisation as a potential organisational psychopath is assessed.

Once policy review and assessments have been completed, a management strategy is formulated to deal with the individual psychopath. The management strategy aims to align the psychopath's self-gratification goals with those of the organisation. Generally a steering committee comprised of stakeholders at various levels within the company are involved in this stage.

Principles identified in human learning psychology are used to shape the intervention plan.

Bill was a very successful sales representative in the communications industry. He achieved record sales on numerous occasions, largely as a result of his smooth talking and a charming manner. He was also an organisational psychopath. He manipulated his staff, lied, displayed no remorse for his behaviours, was sexually promiscuous, bullied junior members of the company and displayed very shallow emotions. However, the fact that he was making large amounts of money for the company could not be ignored by senior management.

It was decided to implement a reinforcement schedule whereby Bill was financially rewarded for positive comments made about him by his co-workers. This encouraged Bill to stop bullying his colleagues. Simultaneously, Bill had monetary bonuses deducted for every employee who resigned from his section and for every customer who complained that they had not received goods as promised. This stopped Bill from lying about his products to increase sales.

In addition, the company removed any authority he had over other workers, and conducted a 360 degree review of his behaviour toward co-workers every six months. Bill was made aware that if he scored very poorly on this 360 degree review he would be dismissed from the company. Initially he tried to bully his subordinates into rating him favourably, but when this was reported to management he realised that his bullying behaviour had to cease. Bill was still manipulative and charming, however he worked within the limitations imposed on his behaviour as the rewards were worth it in terms of self-gratification. He became manageable rather than a problem employee.

The next component of the organisational psychopath management plan is to inoculate the people around the psychopath as much as possible by educating them about how the organisational psychopath operates. Moreover, team building programs are implemented that make it more difficult for the workplace psychopath to isolate and victimise any one person. Potential victims of the psychopath are shown stress management techniques as well as how to recognise the symptoms of depression, anxiety, anger, etc. This is to ensure they recognise when to seek professional intervention. This management stage is based on principles identified in forensic, clinical and organisational psychology.

A medium-sized company was experiencing a problem with a manager who had been identified as an organisational psychopath. The most significant problem, amongst many others, was the high number of staff resigning from the company. Exit surveys were conducted and former staff members reported having low self-esteem, feeling isolated, powerless, lack of job satisfaction, anxiety and depression, to name a few things. A strategy was implemented to manage the psychopath's behaviour, and staff were educated about aspects of forensic psychology. This education focused specifically on characteristics of the organisational psychopath and the potential impact of such people on colleagues.

Employees were also exposed to various stress-management techniques and information about how to deal with a range of difficult situations. Teamwork was explored in the context of uniting the employees so that they did not allow the psychopath to victimise an individual team member with the silent co-operation of other team members. The team building exercises had the additional benefit of increasing productivity because workers felt better about their jobs and the people they worked with. Staff turnover rates fell dramatically, and eventually the organisational psychopath became frustrated with the situation and moved to another company.

The individual psychopath management and team education components of the management strategy are implemented simultaneously to minimise the impact of the psychopath on both company profits and co-workers' mental health in the shortest possible time frame. However, the 'solution' to the organisational psychopath is not a 'quick-fix'. It is generally a lengthy and complicated process that requires commitment from the organisation and its employees.

Even if the psychopath is dismissed or resigns from the organisation, it is still vital to apply some elements of the employee education phase to minimise damage to the psychopath's colleagues. The long-term damage potentially caused by the psychopath must be addressed even after they no longer directly affect their victim's lives. This is true for all four sub-types of psychopath, as each can cause significant psychological trauma for their victims.

Each aspect of the organisational psychopath management plan will be examined in more detail below.

Getting started – tips for protecting the company

If the psychopath is not addressed in the long term, the organisation will be seen as undesirable by potential employees, and only people with no other alternative will accept a job there. This can be extremely costly as loyalty to the company becomes non-existent.

The most important cost to the organisation is the loss of their good name. Market and public confidence falls in relation to an organisation's profitability because employees are resigning at unprecedented rates, productivity is in decline, employees are sabotaging work, and legal costs are astronomical as a result of the organisation being sued by former employees. This means less investors, share prices fall, and talented employees seek work elsewhere. In the long run, failure to address the organisational psychopath can result in serious financial damage to an organisation.

To get started on this evaluation process on a big-picture scale, an organisational consultant needs to be brought in. Companies or individuals should not try and take on the organisational psychopath without getting independent advice.

Organisational assessments

An evaluation needs to be done on the cost to the organisation of continuing to employ an organisational psychopath. These costs may include high staff turnover, which means money is continually being spent on recruitment and training, worker's compensation expenses, liability insurance and legal expenses.

Reductions in productivity and staff morale also affect the corporation's bottom line. I have observed situations where employees who are victimised by the psychopath deliberately sabotage work and products made by an organisation. This sabotage is driven by the victim's belief that if the organisation does not care about them (because the organisation is not listening to their concerns about their psychopathic colleague) then why should they care about the organisation. Victims may not produce essential work, deliberately damage machinery so production grinds to a halt, spread information about what a terrible company they work for, etc. Also, there may be an increase in the number of workplace accidents and staff sick days as a result of the increased levels of stress employees are placed under when they are forced to work with an organisational psychopath.

Collaboration
The next step in putting together a management plan is to look at the company policy and how it deals with conflict and dishonest behaviour. From a company point of view this step should not be taken lightly – senior executives, human resources, managers, employees and relevant trade union representatives need to be consulted and involved.

Managing specific organisational psychopaths

It is only when the organisational psychopath is universally recognised in the organisation as a problem that a coherent, well-defined management solution can be implemented successfully. If everyone does not recognise or agree that the psychopath is a problem, the psychopath will use this division between people to manipulate the situation in their own favour.

Even if the organisational psychopath is recognised as a problem (and this does not always occur by any means), handling them is a difficult proposition at best because they do not want 'help' to improve their behaviour. For them, life and work are all about self-gratification. They have absolutely no reason to change their behaviour because people are not happy with the way they are acting. Instead, they continue to use their tactics to have the person or people who are criticising them suffer from extreme levels of stress and eventual 'nervous breakdown'. The organisational psychopath will try and eliminate the problem employee in any way that they can.

Strategies used by individuals to manage the organisational psychopath differ depending on the victim's work position in relation to the organisational psychopath. If the victim is junior to the psychopath, there is very little they can do on an individual level to manage the psychopath's behaviour. The victim needs to win the support of senior company executives to implement a management strategy that has the backing of the corporation. There is no effective way for an individual to manipulate the psychopath into leaving them alone.

Similarly, a person at the same level as or senior to the organisational psychopath will find it difficult to manage psychopathic behaviour successfully without the support of the corporation. This is particularly true if the organisational psychopath has already damaged the reputation of their boss or colleague. In this situation, where senior executives are supporting the psychopath over the victim, there is no effective way of managing the psychopath's behaviour.

If the organisation recognises they have an organisational psychopath working for them, and if they are committed to dealing with this, certain management strategies can be put in place. These strategies are based upon what are called instrumental learning principles. Instrumental learning is a form of learning based on reinforcing (positively or negatively) and/or punishing behaviours that are either desirable or undesirable.

Positive reinforcement is where a behaviour is rewarded with something that appeals to the person whose behaviour is in question. For example, a child is rewarded with an ice-cream after cleaning his or her room. This means that in future it is more likely that the child will clean his or her room as this is associated with getting an ice-cream. This positive reinforcement also applies to the organisational psychopath, who is motivated by self-gratification. For example, the organisational psychopath will do whatever it takes to make a sale to receive a commission. In the long term making a large number of sales may be followed by a promotion which brings an increase in power over other people in the organisation.

It is very important when managing the psychopath to examine what behaviours the organisational psychopath has previously been rewarded for. Have they been promoted for being ruthless, manipulative and lying? It is common for this to occur. The corporation may have been encouraging the psychopath's behaviour by rewarding it.

Negative reinforcement is where a behaviour is followed by the termination of an unpleasant event. There are two types of learning associated with negative reinforcement, *avoidance learning* and *escape learning*. Avoidance learning occurs when a person prevents an expected negative event from happening, such as putting on sunscreen before going to the beach to stop the negative event of getting sunburned. An organisational psychopath in sales may learn to avoid negative events such as a reduction in their commission for dishonest behaviour by telling the truth about a product and ensuring clients are satisfied.

Jenny is an organisational psychopath who averages $100,000 in sales per month. She consistently makes the most sales in her section, and works on a commission basis of 10 per cent. Jenny also has the highest number of dissatisfied customers, most of whom claim that Jenny lied about what the product was capable of doing. Many of these customers want to return their products, which has the potential of costing the company financially as well as affecting their reputation. A simple learning strategy was put in place to shape Jenny's behaviour.

Jenny was told that for every dissatisfied customer the company determined had been deceived, she would lose $1500 for the sale − $1000 commission and $500 to reimburse the company for expenses. Jenny quickly learned that if she was honest with her customers, and still used her charm to sell products, she was able to average seven sales per month, making $7000. If she lied to customers, she had an average of four customers return their products, which meant that Jenny only made $4000 per month on average after being charged $6000 (four lots of $1500 in penalties) from the total commission of $10,000. It was more financially rewarding for her to be honest about the products she was selling. Jenny avoided the negative event of losing money by being honest with her clients.

Escape learning is a term used to describe how a person learns to escape a situation in order to avoid a negative experience. For example, imagine a noisy airconditioner continually disturbs someone who is trying to sleep. One evening, they get out of bed and kick the airconditioner, stopping the noise. The next time the airconditioner makes a noise, they are likely to kick it because in their mind kicking it causes the noise to stop. In other words, they have learned that behaviour (kicking) stops a negative experience (being disturbed by a noisy airconditioner). In the case of the organisational psychopath, the unpleasant event of being constantly monitored and placed on probation for bullying is terminated when they change their behaviour and stop bullying co-workers. They learn that termination of an unpleasant event (being on probation and constantly monitored) is associated with stopping their bullying behaviour.

When trying to change a person's negative behaviour, particularly the organisational psychopath, punishment is instinctively the most obvious approach. However, punishment is different to positive/negative reinforcement because it is less effective in shaping or changing a person's behaviour. Punishment can involve a negative consequence for a behaviour, such as a child being spanked for swearing. In the case of the organisational psychopath, they may be fined each time they are found to be taking credit for work done by a colleague. Punishment can also involve the removal of a reward when a person does an unfavourable behaviour. For example, an organisational psychopath could be demoted from an 'acting management' role as a result of behaviour that is seen as undesirable by their employer.

One learning approach that has proved to be successful in the management of the organisational psychopath is the use of a system known as the 'token economy'. 'Token economies' work on reinforcing appropriate behaviour while simultaneously punishing undesirable behaviour through the use of 'tokens' or rewards that 'buy' certain things. How this works on the organisational psychopath's behaviour is quite simple. Knowing that an organisational psychopath desires power and influence (promotion) and financial rewards (pay increases) can be used as a reward system – like an old-fashioned gold star chart. Tokens or reward points are earned by the psychopath for behaviour that appeals to them (for example, large sales equals big commission) and also works to the benefit of others (favourable ratings by staff, good customer feedback, and so on). Reward points are deducted for behaviours such as staff complaints, bullying co-workers, failing to attend meetings, etc. The criteria for awarding or deducting points is set by the organisation based on what they feel is important to the company. The psychopath is told that under a performance management scheme they will be promoted and/or receive a pay increase (or other goals that would gratify the psychopath) when they get a certain number of reward points.

Because the psychopath is easily bored and lacks motivation for long-term planning, short-term benefits for achieving a certain number of 'reward points', such as days off work, movie tickets, golf days, is a good thing to implement. Other employees should also be able to earn similar rewards for good work so that they do not see the psychopath being treated as 'special' by the organisation.

A learning-based management program does not change the fact that the employee is an organisational psychopath. Instead, it seeks to reduce staff distress, increase productivity, decrease client dissatisfaction, and reduce staff turnover rates by managing the organisational psychopath's behaviour.

There are also a number of specific day-to-day management tactics that can be used in conjunction with a psychopath management plan.

Day-to-day management strategies for the organisational psychopath

- In addition to planned meetings, visit the psychopath in their office/workspace unannounced. This creates the feeling that they are being monitored and makes them less inclined to flagrantly disregard the rules.
- If the organisational psychopath insists on meeting with you repeatedly simply to inconvenience you, schedule these meetings for just before the psychopath wants to go home. If this does not seem to affect the psychopath, try and make sure that the meetings run well beyond the organisational psychopath's scheduled finish time.
- Plan management sessions very carefully. Understand the objectives of the session, and make sure that these objectives are addressed specifically and succinctly. Have the organisational psychopath commit to the goals of the management program in writing so they are unable to later claim ignorance. Think about possible rebuttals from the workplace psychopath to points in the management plan and have answers ready to counter them.
- If the organisational psychopath appears to become 'emotional' during a meeting, wait for them to calm down. If this does not happen, reschedule the

meeting. If they use the 'emotional' tactic again, address the management criteria in writing, verifying that they have received the written document and requesting a response within a very specific time frame. Emphasise that if they do not respond, obviously they do not take the company seriously and it may be appropriate for them to seek employment elsewhere.

- Do not allow the organisational psychopath to sidetrack the management discussion. Have a written list of points to be addressed and do not deviate from these points for any reason. It is almost certain that the psychopath will attempt to sidetrack the discussion to prevent being restricted by the management criteria.

- If the organisational psychopath arrives late to work or takes days off after the management meeting, make sure they are instructed in writing to ring you and explain why they are absent each time. Record these answers and compare them from day to day for consistency. Also watch for patterns in these absences (for example Mondays and Fridays).

- If you hear rumours that you know are untrue, immediately correct them with the truth. It is important to take prompt action, as this will minimise the damage caused by the organisational psychopath's rumours.

- Document everything in writing. This will ensure that the psychopath cannot escape responsibility for his or her behaviours.

- If you are deliberately blamed for not producing work by the workplace psychopath, particularly after implementing or discussing the management strategy, there are a number of options available. Always document the accusation, and ask for the complaint in writing.

- If you are a team leader, make sure that you have the support of your team. If you don't it is possible the psychopath will turn your team against you and undermine the management strategy you are trying to put in place.

- When the management strategy is implemented, you should expect the organisational psychopath to play office politics harder than ever before as they attempt to avoid the conditions imposed by the management strategy. There are a number of things you can do to minimise the impact of these political games. If you are a supervisor or manager, discourage workers who attempt to win your favour over other workers, as this can build resentment. However, it is important not to alienate your employees at the same time. Avoid being seen to have personal friendships with subordinates. Make sure that people who play office politics are given enough work to do, and monitor work performance to minimise their time to do 'non-work' related activities. Know where the power lies in your organisation, so that you can consult these people in case the politics get out of control. Always be courteous and friendly with everyone, and never neglect your own office politics self-defence strategy.

Treatment can make them worse

There is no effective treatment for psychopathy because it is a pervasive personality disorder that has taken many years to form. A fundamental assumption of any therapy program is that the person seeking treatment wants help, and is willing to change their behaviours. The psychopath does not seek help because they view their self-gratifying behaviours as fulfilling their needs. In *Without Conscience*, Dr Hare states 'psychopath's don't feel they have psychological or emotional problems, and they see no reason to change their behaviour to conform to societal standards with which they do not agree...they see themselves as superior beings in a hostile, dog eat dog world in which others are competitors for power and resources' (p. 195).

The psychopath rarely if ever seeks treatment voluntarily. It is generally as a result of being caught for some type of crime, or identified as a workplace psychopath. By the time psychopaths are identified, their behaviour and personality patterns are well established. For example, they justify their behaviours by claiming that life is survival of the fittest. Because psychopaths are very skilled at deceiving people, this also applies in therapy. The psychopath is a master at appearing to follow the therapeutic goals so that they receive parole, a promotion, probation, and so on. Getting away with the deception may be reinforcing the psychopaths' belief that people are gullible; even professionals who are supposed to be 'experts' can be fooled by them.

Researchers have found that for some psychopaths, therapy may actually make them worse. This can happen for a number of reasons. In group therapy, where individuals discuss their crimes as well as their thoughts and feelings with other group members, the psychopath may learn new more effective methods for committing future crime. They also discover new ways to rationalise their behaviours, and hear about crime methods that did not work.

Damage control

Damage control can be done on a group and an individual level. Group protection involves educating employees about the characteristics of the workplace psychopath to minimise their chances of being victimised. Team-building exercises are helpful in eliminating the psychopath's ability to isolate individual team members.

By addressing self-confidence and self-esteem issues through life-coaching programs and stress management techniques, an employee's vulnerability to a psychopath's assault is lessened.

Group and individual protection strategies need to be specifically tailored depending upon the exact nature of the workplace psychopath. The strategies can be applied to each of the four sub-types of workplace psychopath.

Employee education

The best way to start dealing with this problem is to talk to employees in general terms about bullying in the workplace. The characteristics of workplace psychopaths can then be elaborated upon in the context of addressing bullying. Discretion is critical when educating employees about the potential threats within their workplace.

It is not necessary to refer to or use the word 'psychopath' at all in these types of education strategies, as the word 'psychopath' conjures images of serial killers and other criminals that cloud the reality of the workplace situation. What is particularly important is that employees recognise the person's behaviour as inappropriate, not whether they can label it as 'psychopathic' or not. The case study below provides an example of one approach to this education and team building strategy.

I was asked by a call-centre to assess why a significant number of staff were resigning from one particular team. Traditionally the call-centre industry has a high staff turnover rate as it is, but in this particular section 70 per cent of staff had resigned in a two-month period. Importantly, the high staff resignation rate coincided with the appointment of Jenny, a new team leader.

After a detailed assessment and psychological profile was completed, I determined that Jenny displayed many behaviours and traits that were characteristic of the organisational psychopath.

I advised the company that the best approach would be to commence an education campaign and team-building exercises to combat the techniques used by this particular organisational psychopath. The education campaign was implemented in conjunction with a strategy that used learning principles to manage Jenny's behaviour.

All team members and team leaders in the call centre (including Jenny) were educated at a staff training day about various types of bullying behaviour and its effects on employees. The personality and behavioural characteristics of the organisational psychopath were also outlined in the context of explaining why certain types of bullying behaviour occur. Moreover, the tactics and strategies used by the organisational psychopath were discussed. This ensured that people recognised what was occurring when Jenny manipulated situations, allowing them to recognise and manage her behaviour.

A separate team building day was held specifically for Jenny's team. This training did not include Jenny. It was explained to her that the team members needed to work together, and sometimes the presence of the team leader had a negative effect on this development process. After the team-building exercises, each team member reported feeling better about their work and their situation. They also reported feeling more comfortable about working with Jenny as they had a network of colleagues they could freely talk to about any problems they were having.

On an individual level, team members were educated about the physiology and psychology of stress, depression and anger. They were also shown how to reduce stress in their lives through some simple stress-management techniques. The call-centre industry is stressful by nature, and the exercises they learned were rated as highly useful not only to cope with Jenny, but also when they were feeling 'burnout' associated with other aspects of their work environment.

Finally, an individual life coaching program was developed with each team member. This coaching program looked at challenging negative or limiting thought patterns, setting realistic and achievable goals, and recognising psychological vulnerabilities that could be played upon by the organisational psychopath.

When the entire intervention program was evaluated after three months, no staff members had resigned, and each reported feeling happier and more in control of their workplace and themselves. None of the team members liked working with Jenny, but they felt they could cope with her behaviours and prevent her from manipulating them or other team members. Their productivity increased, and most important of all they felt valued and believed by the organisation they worked for because senior management had noticed and taken action about dissatisfaction in their section.

Staff education is important because it addresses and eliminates the distressing reactions victims face when dealing with the workplace psychopath. Crucial to strengthening how staff and individuals deal with the psychopath is getting rid of the 'blame' factor where people blame themselves for the destructive behaviour that happens. It stops the vicious cycle of blame and feelings of failure that were seen in Jason's case in Chapter 9.

Education creates an awareness of the existence and reality of the workplace psychopath. This means that the problem is external to the victim and is not seen by them as being their fault.

Team building

The organisational psychopath often exploits existing conflicts between employees, or they will create new ones. They play on the fact that employees tend to work independently, are often self-focused and have hidden agendas concerning their work, may distrust other team members, have disagreements that are not constructive, and they often do not have clear channels of communication. These factors can create conflict and peer pressure to conform with the majority of the group.

A good team-building strategy can encourage interdependence between team members as well as openness and trust. Disagreements are seen as positive and constructive parts of the change process rather than competitions for power between team members. Honest and transparent communication should be encouraged, which then allows for free expression rather than conformity to group expectations. Importantly, conflict resolution procedures need to be set in place so that team members become a unified group rather than a set of independent people. It is this unity that protects employees from the organisational psychopath.

If a consultant is called in, it is important for them to be familiar with the reason for the team-building exercise. Also, it is preferable that they have some knowledge of how the workplace psychopath can effect other employees.

- The consultant meets with the human resources and senior management sections in the organisation. The relevance and usefulness of team building is evaluated, and organisational goals are defined. These goals can include increased productivity, reduced sick days, and protection from the workplace psychopath. Employees should also be allocated to specific teams at this stage of the team-building process. Administrative and evaluation criteria should be established to make sure there is no confusion later. For example, frequency and location of team meetings, performance indicators, feedback procedures, etc should all be discussed.

- The consultant meets and establishes rapport with individual team members. The consultant should acknowledge team members' concerns, uncertainty about the process, and encourage open expression of ideas. Expectations for each team member are also clarified so that each team member knows what is expected of him or her.

- Team members meet as a 'team' for the first time. Team members discuss their needs and wants, and the consultant addresses organisational needs. Issues such as why the team has been formed, goals of the team, and the importance of a unified approach are all discussed in an open forum. If team members have not worked together before, a team building exercise is useful. This 'exercise' may range from solving hypothetical problems in the office to a week-long retreat in the wilderness or learning to SCUBA dive together. It is important that team members develop trust in one another, and know they can count on each other for support in difficult situations.

- A second team meeting is organised after the 'bonding exercise'. Group goals are solidified, team members' questions are clarified, and any resistance from individual team members to the overall goals is explored.
- Ongoing meetings with the team take place where progress is discussed. The reaction of the workplace psychopath to the unified team is also dealt with. Feedback is provided to team members, and the human resources department and senior managers are given feedback about the performance of the team in relation to the workplace psychopath's manipulative strategies.

Employee life coaching and self-esteem maintenance

Life coaching and a self-esteem maintenance program are valuable tools that can be used to protect individual employees from the psychopath's destructive influence. Both of these strategies counteract the effects of the psychopath's attempts to isolate and degrade their victim, as they work on encouraging the victim to take active control of their lives and to see themselves as valuable.

Life coaching programs get employees to look closely at their values, perception of themselves and set goals to enrich their lives. Life coaching encourages the individual to focus on defining personal goals and then working towards achieving them. This moves the person away from focusing on fixing negatives (such as a workplace psychopath) while restoring a belief in themselves and taking control of their lives back.

Life coaching also looks at obstacles that prevent an individual from achieving goals. These obstacles can include fear of the unknown, fear of failure, fear of disapproval and fear of making the wrong decision. Other obstacles to making meaningful and lasting change in response to a workplace psychopath are financial limitations, low self-esteem, lack of decisiveness, habit, lack of skills necessary to make a change, lack of energy, and the needs of other people in a victim's life conflicting with their own needs. A life coach can help the victim to overcome these obstacles by showing a person how to implement a series of smaller, more manageable goals that gradually lead to a more positive change. However, life coaching is only an effective strategy when the organisational psychopath is managed by the organisation. Life coaching is not 'the' solution, it is part of an overall strategy to deal with workplace psychopaths.

Teaching employees about self-esteem maintenance is also a useful strategy because it reduces the victim's vulnerability to the workplace psychopath's tactics. Healthy self-esteem comes from self-acceptance, rather than relying on what other people think of us. This means accepting flaws and perceived imperfections, without believing that these imperfections make us worthless. Moreover, when dealing with the workplace psychopath, it is important to accept that not everyone will approve of or like us. It is also important to challenge negative statements based upon what the victim knows about themself.

One useful approach for psychologically challenging the workplace psychopath's claims is Cognitive Behavioural Therapy, which encourages people to look at the feelings caused by a particular situation. These feelings are looked at closely to identify and recognise the thoughts and beliefs that create these feelings. Any beliefs or thoughts that don't contribute to feeling positive are then questioned. After disputing these unhelpful beliefs, positive action is taken so that these negative beliefs do not affect the quality of one's life. For example:

- *Situation* – Jane has been told by her boss (who is an organisational psychopath) that she is a useless employee and he cannot understand how she was given her job in the first place.
- *Feelings* – Jane feels worthless, she cannot do anything right at work.
- *Thoughts* – My boss thinks I am useless, he hates me, he wishes he did not have to see me everyday.
- *Beliefs* – Because I cannot please my boss I am worthless, useless. I should be liked by my boss. My boss should be happy with my work.
- *Dispute* – I am highly qualified and experienced in my job. I have never had a problem before. I have won awards for my excellent performance in the past. Just because this boss tells me I cannot do my job, does not mean I am useless or worthless. Some people like my work and others don't. People are all different. My boss and I have different expectations about what is 'good work' and that is okay.

- *Positive actions* – Stop focusing on what my boss thinks of me and my work. Relax and focus on getting the job done to a standard that I know is good.

Stress management

Employees are invariably placed under a great deal of stress when they share a workplace with the psychopath. Stress management techniques can be taught to reduce and help manage levels of stress. Like life coaching these techniques are not a complete 'solution' to the workplace psychopath.

There a number of things that can be done to help reduce stress levels and to create a 'stress-resilience'. This includes moderating your physical reactions to stress through relaxation techniques, deep breathing, meditation; building on your physical reserves through regular exercise, a healthy balanced diet and getting plenty of sleep; maintaining your emotional reserves such as managing your time, developing a strong support network of friends and family. Stress management techniques are many and varied. Consult with a psychiatrist, psychologist or a counsellor to find out about techniques that are suitable for the situation.

Should I stay or resign?

It is important to note that once a person realises a workplace psychopath is not able to be controlled or managed easily without the support of their organisation, the best strategy for them is often to leave the workplace and find a new job. It has been recognised in psychology for some time that a stressor (such as a workplace psychopath) that is external to the self and cannot be controlled or predicted poses the greatest psychological danger to a person. I have seen numerous victims who have decided to stay with their employer as a matter of principle, for financial reasons, because they have invested X number of years in the company, because they feel like they could not get another job, etc. These victims are often severely psychologically traumatised.

This is not to say that everyone who encounters a workplace psychopath and has their complaint ignored by an organisation should leave their position. The important question to ask is 'at what point does a person's psychological and physical health become more important than their job?'.

It may not be fair that a person has to leave their job on account of a workplace psychopath making their life unbearable. Unfortunately, the expectation that life should be fair does not match what happens in the real world. For example, is it fair that people born in poor families have higher death rates and less opportunities than children born in wealthy families? Is it fair that in many workplaces you can find talented employees being poorly rewarded for working hard while others in senior positions may lack competence yet be paid significantly more? Even though people may wish the world was always fair, it is not. It is possible to spend a great deal of energy and time dwelling on how unfair the situation is, as opposed to telling oneself that life can be unfair and that it is necessary to move on and find a different place to work.

The ethics of labelling

The workplace psychopath is usually reluctant to be a part of the consulting process. However, it is typical for a consultant to be engaged by the organisation because they have a responsibility to their employees and clients to minimise harm once a problem employee is identified. Therefore the consultant's primary responsibility is to the organisation rather than the specific employee. This is not to say that the psychopath and colleagues of the psychopath do not have rights, just that they must be carefully balanced with the desire of the organisation to eliminate the damage being caused by the psychopath. This is similar to an organisational psychologist who specialises in recruitment testing having a primary responsibility to the organisation employing them, but an additional, secondary responsibility, to the people they are testing on behalf of the organisation.

On most occasions the organisation is not in a position to determine whether the 'problem employee' is in fact a psychopath. Therefore it is imperative that a qualified consultant is employed who can identify the cause of the problem, rather than simply developing a solution that may be based upon an inaccurate diagnosis of 'psychopathy' made by a person in the organisation who is not qualified or experienced enough to make such a diagnosis. Hence the first ethical responsibility for any consultant when managing an organisational psychopath is to establish a valid diagnosis of the problem. Alternative causes of difficult employee behaviour will be examined in detail in Chapter 12.

Once a diagnosis is made, the consultant must then advise the organisation whether the best course of action is to dismiss the psychopath from their job, or implement a management strategy to keep the psychopath's behaviours in check. There is no simple rule used to make this determination, it can only be decided on a case by case basis. However, a careful balance needs to be achieved between the needs of the organisation, the workplace psychopath and all employees.

There are a number of strategies that can be used to limit the damaging effect a workplace psychopath can have on individuals and organisations. These strategies don't stand alone, however, and need to be integrated with different coping and prevention techniques for them to be effective.

11

PROFILING THE PSYCHOPATH AND THE ORGANISATION

MANY OF THE PRINCIPLES used to profile violent and dangerous criminals can be applied to the workplace psychopath. Profiling involves making predictions about a person based on an understanding of their personality and behaviours. These predictions can include how they are likely to behave in different situations, how to best interview them, and unusual or defining characteristics that may help an organisation or person recognise them as a workplace psychopath. There are three main ways psychological profiling can be helpful when dealing with the workplace psychopath.

Profiling the workplace psychopath at recruitment

Profiling principles should guide any recruitment strategies used by an organisation (or recruitment agency). There are techniques that can be used to minimise the risk of hiring a workplace psychopath, and reduce the risk to the workplace or organisation. Identifying the workplace psychopath at this stage is the most economical and efficient way of eliminating this significant workplace problem.

Organisations that use psychometric tests often assume that psychopathy will be detected. This is a dangerous assumption to make as the majority of psychometric tests used do not directly screen for psychopathy, they are general personality and IQ tests. These types of personality tests are relatively easy for the psychopath to fake.

There are other organisations that do not believe psychometric testing is effective. They rely very heavily on interviewing all job applicants to screen for any 'undesirable characteristics'. Unfortunately for these organisations, the psychopath generally interviews very well as they are able to identify and quickly shape their responses to fit what the interviewer is looking for.

Profiling applicants' résumés is the first place to start when detecting the workplace psychopath before they enter a company.

The résumé

The workplace psychopath is an expert at shaping a recruitment panel's impressions by writing their résumé in a certain way. They describe ordinary, mundane achievements as though they are monumental accomplishments, and 'economy with the truth' is a standard. While this is not particular to the psychopath, what is unique is how they will make up previous places of employment and bluff their way through the interview if they are discovered. This raises the question of what a recruitment panel should look for to establish which part of the résumé is truth and which part is fiction?

Depending upon the seniority of the position being filled, a great deal of attention should be placed on the verification process. At the very least, verification should include:

- Asking the applicant to show pay slips from previous employers (to prove that they worked there at the specific time in the position they state in their résumé).

- Specifically asking the applicant if any of the referees or previous employers listed on the résumé are friends or relatives. Do not ring referee's numbers listed on the résumé itself, ring the general switch of a company and ask to be transferred to the person named on the résumé as the referee. Also, ask the switch operator what the referees' position in the company is. Be very wary of mobile phone numbers being used as sole contact points for referees.

- Ask the applicant to describe the physical layout of each place they have worked and then check this information. It is a good idea to visit previous employers headquarters to make sure the previous employer is who the applicant says they are.

- Perform credit checks on the applicant where appropriate to evaluate their financial situation. Dire financial situations do not always bode well for a good employee.

- Check court proceedings/transcript databases for any record of the employee being dismissed or causing problems for a previous employer. Industrial Relations Commission and criminal court proceeding transcripts are of particular importance.

- Be sure to ask the potential employee to provide copies of drivers licence, birth certificate and passport before employing them. Make sure these documents are genuine. Often other documents such as electricity bills, magazine subscriptions, library memberships, and so on are better than the standard identification documents as many identity thieves do not take the time to obtain the 'detail' documents that help prove they are who they say they are.

- Evaluate why the person is applying for the job you have advertised. Is it a pay rise, a promotion, a combination, or something entirely different. If the person does not appear to achieve significant benefits from the job you have advertised compared with their previous job then their motivation needs to be checked. For example, it may be possible that they have been told by their previous employer to leave as they are a 'difficult employee'.

- Double check credentials and qualifications the applicant claims to have with the relevant educational institutions.

- Verify registration with professional associations/ registration bodies where appropriate (for example, is a doctor registered as a medical practitioner or have they been struck off for inappropriate behaviour).

It is just as important to consider what has been left out of a résumé. The workplace psychopath may not want to describe long periods on unemployment benefits, an early career that went sour or being fired by a previous employer. If the applicant claims they were ill or overseas, ask for documentation to check this (medical records/bills, passports with visa stamps, etc). Create a checklist of information that should appear in a résumé. This can include personal information, all previous employers, club memberships, educational qualifications, personal interests, proof of previous achievements. However, regardless of job type, if information identified as important is not in a résumé, the applicant should be asked to provide it or not be awarded the job.

The interview

There are a number of techniques that can be used by recruitment panels to increase their chances of detecting the workplace psychopath at the interview stage.

Each member of the interview panel should be thoroughly familiar with the applicant's résumé. Inconsistencies between what the applicant says and what is written in their résumé should be noted. The applicant should not be allowed to look at or refer to their résumé at any stage during the interview because they should know exactly what it says.

It is important to ask job candidates to describe both positive and negative aspects about themselves. The psychopath may find it difficult to describe negative aspects as they are not sure what the interview panel wants to hear. Gaps in employment, numerous jobs over a short period of time should all be explored. Answers should then be reviewed later for consistency as often the psychopath will not think through a lie they tell.

Pay careful attention to those candidates who look near-perfect on paper. Questions should be asked about their résumé out of sequence (for example, what did they do in the last year, what did they do ten years ago, where were they two years ago, and so on).

Do not have one person doing interviews wherever possible. It is harder for the psychopath to manipulate a panel of people compared with a single person. This is not to say that the psychopath cannot manipulate a panel. They can.

There are some techniques that increase an interview panel's chances of detecting a workplace psychopath. These techniques include:

- Listen carefully and let the applicant do most of the talking.
- Ask the applicant to describe their experience before disclosing information about the position. This prevents them from shaping their experience to what you are looking for.
- Do not be 'dazzled' by unusual or captivating characteristics such as a smooth, soothing voice, rapid talking, intense gaze, theatrical hand-movements.
- Do not evaluate the applicant in terms of whether they are what you are looking for. Instead, try and

find everything about the applicant that does not fit with what you are looking for. This ensures interview panel members are more critical during the interview process, which will decrease the chances of being manipulated.

- If the applicant is appealing to you through flattery, praise and glossing over aspects related to the actual job, be very wary. The psychopath is excellent at making people feel comfortable or good about themselves. This often leads to them being given a job when they do not have the skills.
- If possible, include a professional consultant in the interview panel who is familiar with workplace psychopaths and the interview strategies they use. The independent person is less likely to be deceived by the psychopath because they are looking for specific and objective sets of characteristics.

After the interview, ask the candidate to write a three to four page statement about themselves, their achievements, their family, social life, why they want the job, why they are the best person for the job, physical layout of previous places of employment, who they have worked with, their work ethic, and so on. This criteria should be based on the job characteristics and what the organisation is looking for in potential employees. Don't tell the interview candidates about this before the interview.

They should be given no more than 20 minutes or so to complete this task. This short time frame does not give the psychopath enough time to filter information or plan what they will write.

Once the document has been written by the applicant, it should be analysed by a person experienced in looking for deception in written documents. A technique that has been used widely in profiling is the SCAN or Scientific Content Analysis technique, which points out a number of areas to look at.

If deception is detected in a job applicant's essay about themselves, this does not necessarily mean they are a workplace psychopath. However, it does indicate that increased caution should be used when checking everything else they have said to interviewers. Their résumé should also be double checked.

How do others rate each applicant's behaviour?

Once a small number of potential employees have been identified as a result of the interview process, it is useful to compare each applicant's performance in previous positions before employing them. This performance review does not exclusively focus on productivity or financial worth to a previous employer, it investigates how the person's behaviour is rated by work colleagues.

Specifically, the performance review instrument asks former colleagues from all levels to rate the applicant on a series of questions that relate to the organisational psychopath characteristics described in the earlier chapters of this book. Bosses, senior management, colleagues at the same level, and people junior to the applicant all critique his or her organisational/managerial conduct, interpersonal conduct, and emotional/individual characteristics.

Following is an example of a questionnaire that can be given to as many people who know the job applicant as possible. The questionnaire is very similar to a traditional 360 degree review, however the questions are designed to specifically assess workplace psychopath and antisocial type behaviours in the organisational setting. Scores are tallied at the end. If the applicant scores within a certain pattern or range of scores, this suggests that additional investigation is necessary. Some sample questions from a total of ninety include:

1. Does _____ take responsibility for their behaviour?

2. Has _____ ever played one person against another in your office?

3. Has _____ ever had an affair to your knowledge with a person they work with?

4. Does _____ constantly look for new things to excite them?

5. Would you say that _____ has career aspirations that are realistic?

6. Has _____ ever taken credit for work that you or someone else has done?

7. Has _____ ever been on performance review or some other form of management plan?

8. Is _____ prepared to do whatever it takes to get what they want, regardless of the cost to other people?

9. Would you describe _____ as a good talker?

10. Does _____ ever act without thinking about the consequences of their behaviour?

11. Have you ever felt intimidated by _____?

12. Does _____ ever lose their temper for short periods of time to make people afraid of them?

13. Who do you think is the most important person in _____'s life?

The rationale behind asking people other than the job applicant about previous performance is to get as balanced a view as possible. One drawback of using this questionnaire is that it is sometimes difficult to find previous colleagues who are willing to provide answers. This is not necessarily because the applicant is a workplace psychopath. It may be that the applicant has not informed their employer they are applying for a new job, colleagues may be difficult to find or approach discreetly, and many colleagues simply do not have the time to complete the questionnaire. A good consultant who is experienced in the area should have developed appropriate systems to circumvent these problems.

Profiling the organisation

If a workplace psychopath is found to be employed in an organisation, it is useful to develop a profile that evaluates the organisational response to such a person. An organisational profile examines standard corporate or agency responses where individuals make a report about a colleague being a 'difficult employee' to work with. The organisational profile identifies how effectively the organisational system balances the workplace psychopath's behaviour with other employee's needs. It also looks at the relationship between the organisational response to the workplace psychopath and corporate culture. Organisational profiling charts the typical flow of events that are set in motion when a 'difficult employee' is reported. This profile is important because it can be used to identify organisational shortcomings at different stages.

The organisational profile is also valuable because it identifies companies who are at high risk of being victimised and exploited by the workplace psychopath. Companies with poor organisational procedures and responses to workplace psychopaths are more vulnerable to attack.

Typically the first procedural step is taken when one or more victims report that they are working with a 'difficult' employee. It is usually the case that these reports are not made immediately by the victim because it is a big psychological step for many people to 'dob in' a co-worker, no matter how unpleasant they may be. The victim often tries to cope with the workplace psychopath's attention for a while, but eventually they are worn down by negative treatment they are experiencing and decide to speak to management.

Remember that it is quite possible that this difficult employee is not a psychopath. Instead they may be a person with poor interpersonal skills, low self-esteem, short temper, another personality disorder, and so on.

Unfortunately, irrespective of the diagnosis made of the 'difficult employee', the organisational response is usually the same – inadequate and often dismissive of the victim's concerns. Most organisations have set channels and procedures for complaints, usually involving the human resources section and the immediate supervisor of the complainant (presuming they are not the subject of the complaint). Many victims report that the human resources section often try to make the problem disappear by providing explanations or telling the complainant to 'get on with the job' and stop worrying about personal issues.

Organisational responses to complaints about fellow workers can include:

- 'They (the subject of the complaint) *are just under a lot of pressure, give it time and it will sort itself out.*'
- '*It is your responsibility to work with your colleagues, if this is not possible it may be more appropriate for you to find work elsewhere.*'
- 'They (the subject of the complaint) *have been identified as a potential future leader of the company,* we (the human resources department and/or senior management) *find it difficult to believe the allegations made.*'

- *'There are always going to be conflicts and different personalities on any team, this is an unfortunate fact of life.'*
- *'After looking into the allegations made, we have concluded that it is inappropriate for the human resources section to become involved in personal matters of the nature raised in your letter.'*
- *'We will endeavour to look into the matter and you will be informed if and when any action is taken.'* (No action follows and the complainant never hears about the matter again until they write another complaint.)
- *'The organisation retains an organisational psychology firm that you may wish to see if you cannot handle the pressure of your position.'*
- *'We have looked into the allegations made and find no substance to them. We are very happy with the performance of* (the difficult employee) *and advise you against making further complaints. A record of your inability to work with* (the difficult employee) *may be recorded on your personnel file in future instances.'*

A common procedure when a complaint is made about a person in an organisation is to allow the subject of the complaint to respond to any allegations made. When a workplace psychopath is involved, this procedure alerts the psychopath to the fact that someone in the organisation is 'brave' or 'stupid' enough to make a complaint about them. Some organisations are not careful enough at protecting the identity of the complainant, and the workplace psychopath finds out who they are. Alternatively, the workplace psychopath can use their extensive network in the company to discover who has made the complaint.

When the psychopath finds out who made the complaint, their victim's life is made unbearable as the psychopath does all they can to force that person to leave or retract the complaint. At this point, the employees in the company are often forced to choose sides, stick with the workplace psychopath and be 'protected' or go against them and become another target. Generally people who are not directly involved try and do everything possible to stay that way. This protects the psychopath's position and weakens the victim's position by socially isolating them. Morale usually drops, as does productivity and the generation of new ideas because no one wants to stand out in such a climate of fear and uncertainty. People often tell the victim privately that they agree with what they are doing, but do not publicly condemn the psychopath for their behaviour. This further increases the sense of isolation and frustration felt by the victim.

The final stage is where the complainant either resigns, goes public with their complaints or takes legal action against the organisation for failure to protect them from the psychopath.

If the complainant resigns quietly, the organisation usually does nothing more unless larger numbers of people resign and high staff resignation rates become a financial consideration. This approach protects the psychopath's position, and can result in the organisation developing a reputation as a bad place to work.

The organisational culture becomes one of fear, mistrust, and uncertainty rather than one of teamwork and cooperation associated with high productivity and job satisfaction.

If an employee goes public or takes legal action, the situation becomes unfavourable from a public relations point of view. If the situation reaches this stage, it has become one of crisis management rather than an employee management problem. This means that the financial ramifications for the company are far more significant because the effects of the situation are felt at every level of the organisation.

Organisational profiling allows the organisation to assess their response at each of these stages, minimising the chances that the situation will go from employee management to crisis management by implementing appropriate strategies at each stage.

Profiling the workplace psychopath within an organisation

Psychological profiling can be useful to identify workplace psychopaths and guide strategies to manage their behaviour. Descriptive characteristics of organisational, corporate criminal, violent criminal, and occupational psychopaths can be used to identify potential workplace psychopaths and alert co-workers and clients to a potential problem employee. This third area of profiling is the most widely used when organisations believe they have employed a workplace psychopath.

The following characteristics should not be used to diagnose a person as any of the four sub-types of workplace psychopath. Rather, they indicate a need for further investigation into the 'difficult' or 'problem' employee by appropriately qualified and experienced experts. Moreover, the characteristics and behaviours described here are by no means an exhaustive list or definitive guide for identifying workplace psychopaths. The information on characteristics mentioned here should be used as guidelines and not used to make claims that a person is a workplace psychopath.

Profiling the organisational psychopath

The criteria presented in Chapter 4 of this book are the general characteristics one would expect to see in an organisational psychopath. However, for people working with the organisational psychopath, it is not always possible to observe these characteristics on a daily basis. This section provides some examples of behaviours that co-workers may observe in an organisational psychopath. The criteria presented below are usually associated with the strategies employed by the organisational psychopath also described in Chapter 4.

The greater the number of behaviours displayed by the person of interest, the more urgent the need for a prompt and thorough investigation by an independent consultant. If multiple behaviours are observed, at the very least an internal assessment by the human resources department must be conducted.

Behaviours to be aware of include but are not limited to:
- Humiliates a person in public by shouting at them, temper tantrums, ridicule of work or physical disability.

- Maliciously spreads lies about a person to discredit their reputation in the organisation.
- Displays no remorse or guilt for their behaviour.
- Frequently lies.
- Rapidly shifts between emotions to manipulate people or cause high levels of fear.
- Ignores a person to isolate them from organisational resources and support systems. This makes the victim feel socially isolated and helpless, increasing their vulnerability.
- Accuses a person of making mistakes or not completing work when the accuser knows what they are saying is unfounded. This works to humiliate or shift blame away from the organisational psychopath who has failed to complete the work.
- Encourages co-workers to torment, harass and humiliate a fellow co-worker.
- Taking credit for other people's work.
- Steals or sabotages a person's work so that the person is disciplined or embarrassed about completing assigned tasks.
- Refuses to accept responsibility.
- Uses the threats of job loss, disciplinary action, 'black marks' on personnel files as a way of intimidating others.
- Sets unachievable tasks for employees to set them up for failure and allowing disciplinary action to be taken by them on behalf of the organisation.
- Refuses to attend meetings when more than one person will be there as they do not want to be

accused of not performing without being able to blame someone else.

- Refuses to provide adequate training to a victim who has been singled out or targeted.
- Invades the personal privacy of others by going through files, emails, desk contents.
- Has multiple sexual encounters with junior and/or senior employees.
- Develops new ideas and never follows through. Often these new ideas are given to someone at the last minute and the organisational psychopath will blame them when the new idea fails.
- Self-focused, talk about themselves, act self-important, believe the world revolves around them.
- May borrow sums of money from co-workers with no intention of ever repaying this money.
- Does whatever it takes to secure a contract or deal, regardless of how unethical or illegal the behaviour may be.

Profiling the corporate criminal psychopath

Here are some behaviours to be aware of for the corporate criminal psychopath. For more detailed information see Chapter 5. People with a combination of the psychopathy characteristics and the behaviours listed below are more likely to be white-collar corporate criminal psychopaths:

- Works unusually long hours.
- Resists being promoted out of their current position.

- Refuses to take annual leave.
- Purchases things that are obviously above their salary level such as luxury cars or overseas trips.
- Sudden changes in spending habits or lifestyle.
- Frequent unexplained absences from work.
- Missing or altered company records of financial transactions are associated with their work.
- Excessive billing expenses in relation to the work done.
- Establishes very close relationships with clients or accounts staff responsible for clients.
- Does excessive overtime.
- The same billing address for different accounts managed by the same person.
- Frequently ignores internal company policy for accounting systems.
- Does 'creative' bookkeeping to make sure everything balances for the auditors.
- Ignores management requests to justify particular financial irregularities as they are 'too busy' to waste time.

Profiling the violent criminal psychopath

Profiling the violent criminal psychopath is a little different to profiling other types of workplace psychopath. This is because the violent criminal psychopath does not always attack people they work with, therefore colleagues may be completely unaware that any violent behaviour has occurred. Though the chance of a co-worker recognising a violent criminal psychopath is very small, public tip-offs to the police about people suspected of being violent criminal psychopaths have been known to solve cases.

Psychological profilers assist police to develop a criminal profile that describes an unknown violent criminal psychopath. Criminal profiling has been made popular in recent years through such films and TV programs as *Silence of the Lambs*, *Copycat* and *Profiler*, however the reality of criminal profiling is very different. So what exactly does criminal profiling do?

First, it can provide police with a personality and behavioural profile of an unknown offender so that investigators have a better idea of what sort of violent criminal psychopath they are dealing with.

Second, a profiler recommends investigation strategies that may decrease the amount of time taken to identify and apprehend an offender, reducing the number of crimes committed by that offender.

Third, a profiler can develop guidelines for interviewing the violent criminal psychopath once they have been caught. The interview strategy maximises investigators' chances of eliciting information from a suspect as they know 'what buttons to push' when it comes to talking to an offender. For example, some offenders respond to the confrontational approach whereas others are more likely to open up when more subtle 'non-confrontational' tactics are used.

Finally, criminal profiling can be used to develop a risk assessment for a victim who is receiving unwanted attention from either a known or unknown offender. For example, a profiler may evaluate a person working for a particular employer in relation to the potential for workplace violence to occur. This technique has been used in the United States where profilers do risk assessments or 'threat assessments' for organisations. These risk assessments evaluate if the organisation is a high or low risk target. The profiler then recommends strategies to manage the potential threat.

Based on a clinical profiling model from the United Kingdom, a number of stages are used to compile a profile of a particular offender.

The first step in any profile is to receive a detailed briefing from the client. This is usually a law enforcement agency, a corporation or an individual who is the subject of 'unusual' behaviour. All case material is analysed by the profiler at this stage.

For example, I was contacted by an organisation who were worried that one of their employees was being stalked by a co-worker. They presented me with a detailed list of all incidents recorded by the victim over a four-month period, as well as a list of co-workers and any personnel files that seemed relevant.

The next step is to visit the crime scene. This visit is crucial to help understand the context and importance of case materials. The crime scene may be where a murder victim's body has been found, the scene of a sexual assault, or the victim's house and workplace.

In this case, the victim's house was located in a relatively isolated area surrounded by dense bush. There were multiple sites a person could use to observe the victim going about her daily activities at home without her being aware of their presence. At her workplace, security was generally poor when it came to building access, and anyone could watch where the victim parked her vehicle each day.

The profiler then undertakes the most important step in the profiling process; inferring motivation behind the offence from case materials presented. The profiler reconstructs the sequence of events that have occurred based on the case materials. Then they examine what has happened, how the sequence of events has happened, and to whom (victimology) the events have happened.

In the stalking case, events were reconstructed in minute detail by going through each incident recorded by the victim and examining exactly what occurred. Time of day, location, frequency of offender behaviour, type of offender behaviour, etc, were all examined. Where and when the offender was likely to target the victim were analysed for any pattern. The victim risk level was also examined, as was her lifestyle and previous history. In this example, this victim was at low risk of attracting the attention of a stalker. However, the ease with which a person could observe her movements increased her risk slightly. The fact that the victim was unaware of what precautions to take or what to look for when being followed further elevated her risk.

Specific incidents that the victim experienced included frequent telephone calls where a male voice (not recognised by the victim) told her he wanted to perform various sexual acts with her, asked her if she loved him, told her he loved her, etc. The telephone calls were received at home, on her mobile phone, and at work. The offender seemed to be physically observing the victim as a call would be received at home just after the victim walked through the front door. The victim also had underwear stolen from her clothesline, keys went missing from inside her house, her car was tampered with and moved from one parking space to another close by, and she heard a prowler in the early hours of the morning outside her bedroom window on multiple occasions.

She also received flowers, cards, letters and chocolates from an anonymous person while she was at work, and items had been moved on her desk while she was not there. The letters became more explicit over the four months, as the stalker began to suggest sexual behaviours he was interested in. The stalker also began to question why the victim kept on rejecting him, did she think he was not good enough for her?

From each of these behaviours, the motive of the offender is inferred. In this case, the stalker appeared to be a love-obsessional stalker who wanted to have a relationship with the victim. This was evident from the letters, 'romantic' acts such as flowers and chocolates, and the attempts by the stalker to 'contact' the victim. The stalker's willingness to share his sexual fantasies with the victim further supported this inferred motive. I was worried about the victim risk in this case as the stalker was obviously violating the law. Also, the stalker's frustration with the victim for not reciprocating his 'love' further elevated victim risk in my opinion, as it is not unknown for these stalkers to take by force what they want and sexually assault the victim. This would be similar to the power-reassurance rapist covered in Chapter 6. The risk assessment was based upon what is known about these types of stalkers both from the literature and experience profiling other similar cases.

Once a risk assessment is complete, psychological characteristics of the offender are inferred. In the stalking case, the offender was likely to be a person who knew the victim, though the victim did not necessarily know the offender. For example, the offender could be a client, or a co-worker in a different section who the victim has seen but does not know well. On the other hand, the offender would 'know' the victim as it was most likely he had been following her for a considerable period of time. The offender had obviously devoted a great deal of time and energy toward following the victim. A clinical profiler would look at degree of planning, cognition and affect (thoughts and emotions) experienced by the offender, as well as themes of power, anger and control demonstrated in the offender's behaviour. The presence of any possible mental illness is also evaluated.

I advised the organisation that the potential was definitely there for the victim to be sexually assaulted at some stage if the stalker's behaviour continued to intensify. Moreover, it was unlikely that the stalking behaviour was going to stop in the near future. The victim was becoming increasingly frightened by the offender's actions. One of the most important aspects of the profile was that as the offender would be following the victim, he would not necessarily be aware of counter-surveillance measures. The organisation hired a security specialist to follow the victim at a discreet distance and observe whether any one person seemed to be near her on multiple occasions. It turned out that a male who worked in the same organisation as the victim also shopped in the same place at the same time as the victim, left work at the same time as the victim without fail, drove around her neighbour-hood in the early hours of the morning, and went to florists on the same days as the victim received flowers from the anonymous stalker (the stalker liked to pick the flowers personally).

The personality profile of the stalker lead to an effec-tive investigative strategy that resulted in him being identified. The stalker was married with children, but had become obsessed with the victim after he had seen her at work. He believed she was his soul mate and that everything he did was justified because in his mind people have to work hard to win their soul mate's heart. Against my advice, the victim decided she did not want police action as long as the organisation disciplined the stalker and he promised to stop the stalking behaviour. The stalker was disciplined and the stalking behaviour stopped for a short period of time. Regrettably, the victim was physically assaulted by the stalker a few months later and he was charged by the police.

Profiling the occupational psychopath

The occupational psychopath is more difficult to observe based on behaviour when compared to the other types of workplace psychopath. This is because they prey on vulnerable people who are lost in the system or ignored by the very people who are supposed to protect them. Here are some behaviours to be aware of for this sub-type:

- High numbers of complaints about the person from clients and co-workers.
- Secretive behaviours or a feeling that no one knows what the individual is working on at any one time.
- Secretive about their movements and work activities, and provides very general responses when questioned.
- Rarely takes time off from work as they enjoy the access it gives them to victims.

For more detailed information see Chapter 7.

Calling in the professionals

There are a number of consultants with different backgrounds who can help any organisation interested in profiling and managing the psychopath.

Forensic psychology/psychiatry consultant

A forensic psychologist or psychiatrist is the only person who is able to reliably and validly diagnose a person as a psychopath or antisocial personality disordered. A forensic psychologist or psychiatrist is a person with training in understanding criminal and antisocial behaviour (including sub-criminal or non-criminal psychopaths). They should be the first person consulted when an organisation believes they may have employed a workplace psychopath.

It is important to check that the consultant is experienced at evaluating psychopathy, particularly in the workplace. This is the best person to work with the management team when putting in place strategies to manage or deal with a psychopathic employee because they understand how the workplace psychopath thinks.

It is also important to make sure that any forensic psychologist or psychiatrist is experienced with psychological profiling techniques for both criminal and non-criminal psychopaths.

Even though a forensic psychologist/psychiatrist can recommend strategies to improve the workplace, they cannot implement them. Their suggestions need to be drafted by a lawyer to take into account industrial relations law, workplace legislation and other relevant legal matters.

When hiring a forensic psychologist or psychiatric consultant make sure you feel they thoroughly understand your needs and have the knowledge and experience to deal with your problem.

Management consultants

A management consultant plays a secondary role in looking at employee performance issues as a result of the psychopath's behaviour. They can evaluate corporate structures and systems that are in place to deal with a psychopath.

Ex-law enforcement/security consultants

Ex-police officers and security consultants are ideal for investigating and proving or disproving allegations made against an employee. They can help detect fraud and criminal behaviours. These are the best professionals to call in once the psychopath has been identified by a qualified forensic psychologist or psychiatrist. However, they are not so good at understanding the psychology underlying the workplace psychopath because this is not always relevant in an investigation. Therefore they are of very limited use when it comes to screening at recruitment, profiling, and managing the psychopath from a strategic viewpoint.

Lawyers

A lawyer can draft legal agreements to make sure that employees who leave corporations do not leak confidential information about the company. This limits the potential long-term damage caused by the psychopath. They can draft corporate policies and are useful when an organisation is confronted by legal action from either the workplace psychopath or victims of a workplace psychopath.

Recruitment firms

A recruitment firm should be instrumental in screening for psychopathy. Unfortunately, the majority of recruitment firms do not have the relevant skills to deal specifically with the workplace psychopath. Recruitment firms need to work with the forensic psychologist/psychiatrist and develop appropriate screening techniques for the organisation.

Human resources department

This department in any organisation should play a pivotal role when dealing with the workplace psychopath. They should be the first contact point for the victims. However, many Human Resources managers are unaware of the workplace psychopath, and are unable to deal with the problem effectively. The human resources department should implement policy guidelines dealing with the workplace psychopath promptly and effectively, and in collaboration with the other types of consultants previously mentioned. The human resources department should also make sure that employee counsellors are experienced when it comes to counselling victims of the workplace psychopath.

Forensic accountants

Forensic accountants have obvious value when it comes to detecting the corporate criminal psychopath. A forensic accountant is an accountant who specialises in examining company records looking for anomalies that may indicate a fraud has taken place. However, they are also valuable when it comes to detecting the other sub-types of workplace psychopath because each sub-type is prone to stealing from the organisation or 'cooking the books' in some way if there is an advantage for them.

From a practical viewpoint, none of the above consultants are any more important or effective than any other. What is important is that they are employed as a team to implement the best possible policy based upon an understanding of the workplace psychopath's psychology.

12

MISTAKEN IDENTITY –
ALTERNATIVE DIAGNOSES

FOR EVERY BAD MANAGER, co-worker or client who is a
workplace psychopath, there are many others who are
not. In fact the majority of 'dysfunctional employees'
are not psychopaths. There are a variety of alternative
explanations for difficult or impossible workplace
behaviours. Reasons can include lack of management/
leadership training, low self-esteem, inability to cope
with stress, inadequate communication skills, rela-
tionship/family problems, mental illnesses such as
personality disorders, schizophrenia, and drug, alcohol
or gambling addictions.

These alternate diagnoses still produce a manager,
co-worker or client who makes life at work unbearable.
The fact that the person is not a psychopath gives little
comfort to the people experiencing the psychological
and sometimes physical injury. Fortunately, many of
the alternate diagnoses for dysfunctional workplace

behaviour can be recognised and managed more easily than psychopathy.

Poor interpersonal skills – the over-controlling boss

One of the most common explanations for a manager or boss being mistakenly labelled a psychopath is poor interpersonal skills. Many managers who have poor interpersonal skills frequently 'over-control' their employees in an attempt to manage a situation they feel they have no control over. This over-control or 'intrusive supervision' alienates employees, which creates resentment, which causes the manager to become more and more frustrated about their lack of control over their staff. A vicious cycle is set up as the manager tries to re-assert their dominance, only to be faced with unhappy staff. Eventually either the manager cracks or the employees are transferred or resign after putting up with a great deal of physical and psychological stress.

David had worked for the government for twenty-five years, and he was finally promoted to a senior management position where he was responsible for 135 employees. He did not receive training in leadership or communication skills as it was assumed he had picked up these abilities throughout his twenty-five years of service.

In his first month as senior manager, he succeeded in alienating the majority of his employees as he attempted to assert his authority over the department. He changed their working hours without consultation, told employees he was not interested in their input. He said his department was not a democracy, giving orders to be followed not questioned. The employees complained to others which made David look like a bad manager who could not handle his staff. David reacted to this by clamping down even more, emphasising trivial rules and regulations that had not been followed for many years.

After David's boss reviewed his management style, it was suggested that David attend executive coaching and communication skills sessions. In these sessions David revealed that he was anxious about his new position, he had never been shown how to work with people because he had always experienced a hierarchical system in which employees 'followed orders'. Once he understood that over-controlling employees did not lead to productive workers, he was willing to change his approach. David now understands that leadership is not equal to control over people, but is about earning people's respect rather than demanding it.

Generally the over-controlling manager thinks about their employees and their job in a relatively predictable and limited way. Often they have a big workload (either in reality or in their own minds) and this causes them to feel tense, anxious and sometimes angry as they are not sure if they can cope. They sometimes resent the people who have given them the work. This resentment is often taken out on their subordinates.

Importantly, many over-controlling managers believe that all of the work has to be done perfectly by their employees because the quality of the work done is a direct reflection of their ability as a manager. If the work done by their employees is good, they look good as a manager and will get their next promotion. Therefore they reason that they have to monitor everything their employees do to guarantee that the work is perfect. Some of the thoughts that over-controlling managers have about their employees include:

- If I don't fight for people to do their work then nothing will get done.
- People can't be relied on to do the job right.
- If I don't stay right on top of them, it is going to be a complete and utter disaster.
- If this job is not done exactly how I want it done, it means that I am not a good manager.
- I don't have time to delegate jobs, it is faster to tell people how I want it done. That is what a manager does, isn't it?

Clearly these thoughts about employees and the work environment influence the over-controlling manager's behaviour. These thoughts also influence how the over-controlling manager interprets things that happen at work. When the over-controlling manager tells an employee how to do a job, and the job is then completed correctly, the over-controlling manager attributes this success to his or her management style. This means that in future they will continue to be over-controlling because it has worked in the past. Any resentment from their employees is interpreted as inability on the part of employees to cope with the stresses and pressures of their job. The over-controlling manager does not see that employee stress or reactionary behaviour might be caused by their own management style.

The over-controlling manager justifies his or her behaviour through the following beliefs about employees and appropriate workplace behaviours:

- You must know your place in the hierarchy, someday you too will be able to 'manage' other people.
- You must never challenge decisions I make about issues as this is costly and shows a lack of respect.
- You must not make decisions for yourself, employees cannot be trusted to do this until they have proven themselves, at which point they will be given a more senior role.
- Even though I delegate responsibility for certain things to you, everything you do showcases my ability as a manager, therefore I must personally approve everything that you do.

The beliefs held by the over-controlling manager need to be challenged, as does the validity of his or her conviction that they are the only person with the ability to complete a particular job. One of the most important aspects in this boss/employee relationship is the ability to communicate effectively. Communication skills such as the ability and willingness to listen, empathising with employees, and exchanging ideas clearly establishes a climate of trust.

Many managers and employees consider themselves to be good listeners, when the reality is usually the reverse. Some organisational psychologists claim that poor listening skills are the greatest source of conflict between managers and employees. Good listening involves thinking about what the other person is saying, asking relevant questions and reaching conclusions. The primary purpose of listening is to understand another person's point of view. If managers and employees worked toward this goal, and 'really' listened to each other, many conflicts could be avoided in the first place. A good psychologist should be able to coach a person in the art of effective communication.

The famous Type-A, B, C and D personalities

Different personality types often clash in the workplace, leading to conflict that has nothing to do with psychopathy. A major factor that differentiates between a personality clash from psychopathy is the psychopath's lack of remorse as well as experiencing pleasure from any psychological and/or physical injury caused to the victim.

There are many theories of personality, ranging from Freud's psychodynamic approach to Maslow's theory of self-actualisation and Skinner's behaviourism. One of the more popular theories used in the business world involves four personality types: A, B, C, and D. Not all personality types get along, and there are specific ways to deal with each personality type to help minimise workplace conflict.

The Type-A personality is a spontaneous, achievement driven person who is up-front, persuasive and a risk taker. This personality type is generally highly competitive and self-assured. People who work with these people may see them as aggressive and too competitive in going after what they want. The other traits of this type can often be interpreted as domineering, manipulative, pushy, impatient, arrogant and controlling. The Type-A personality dislikes people who are not fast and decisive, particularly those people who follow the rules to the letter. If you are working with or for a Type-A personality make sure positive feedback is given regularly and you are up-front and honest about what you want, you are always enthusiastic, recognise the importance of their work and encourage them to use their creative abilities.

The Type-B personality is a task-oriented person who must always win. This personality type takes charge and would describe themselves as practical, ambitious, methodical, efficient, direct, results-oriented, determined and conventional. The Type-B personality dislikes people who are ambiguous about what they want, who become emotional about practical matters, and people they believe are lazy. The Type-B personality can be seen by others as frugal, uncaring, distant, stubborn, aloof, uncompromising, and inflexible.

If you are working with or for a Type-B personality, make sure they are given as much control over their work as possible, are allowed to use their organisational abilities, are given challenging work, and their efficient and practical way of doing things is taken on board by co-workers. If they are your manager or boss, it is helpful to be clear and to the point, respect their authority, focus on results (these types want results rather than a long-winded explanation about why you could not finish something), follow their rules and regulations, and logically explain alternative ways of doing things.

The Type-C personality has a strong desire to help other people. This personality type keeps stress bottled up, and are often victims of the workplace psychopath rather than difficult employees to work with. They are generally trustworthy, enthusiastic, sensitive, approachable, good listeners, warm and outgoing, are often protective of people who are being victimised and want people to like them.

The Type-D personality is detail-oriented as opposed to having good interpersonal skills. They enjoy working alone, and can often be found in accounting, engineering, technical and other similar professions. They could be described as rigid, meticulous, accurate, strict rule followers and risk avoiders. Their approach could be characterised by people in conflict with them as boring, uninspiring, monotonous, anti-change, unsociable and a perfectionist. If you are working with or for the Type-D personality keep in mind that they respond to hard facts and data, consistency, detailed documentation of ideas and the work completed. They work within deadlines, and expect employees to do the same. They are also the type of person who will demand respect simply because they are the manager of a particular section.

No one could figure out how Ian had got a managerial position in the public service. He seemed to have no personality and was rigid and difficult to get along with. He dismissed his employees' concerns without really listening to them. He applied the rules and regulations and did not tolerate his decisions being questioned. Ian rarely communicated verbally, he preferred to send his answers in the form of an official letter. This practice further alienated employees who 'answered to him'.

Ian was clearly of only average intelligence and had worked his way up to his present position through years of service rather than ability. He thought that his employees viewed him as an efficient and valuable member of the public service. He had no insight into the fact that his lack of social skills alienated the vast majority of employees. He was simply a Type-D personality who was so focused on getting the job done within the confines of a detailed set of rules that he did not think about how his social skills affected the people around him.

Passive-aggressive personality

Passive-aggressive people show a pattern of negative attitudes and passive resistance to demands for adequate performance in social and occupational settings. Passive resistance to working effectively can include such behaviours as forgetfulness, stubbornness, procrastination and intentional inefficiency or working deliberately slowly. These individuals channel their aggression into passive forms of resistance by slowing down the efforts of others, which is frustrating in many ways. The passive-aggressive personality can be quite difficult to detect, and many people do not know why they feel frustrated when dealing with these types because they do not do anything overt to cause this frustration. The passive-aggressive employee can be summed up as a person who obstructs the efforts of others by deliberately failing to do their share of work.

For example, a passive-aggressive employee may be given a presentation to prepare for their boss by a set date. The individual will not prepare the presentation, but will tell their boss it is ready right up until the day of the presentation. At this point, the boss is unable to give the presentation and looks like a failure.

The passive-aggressive person often feels cheated, unappreciated, misunderstood, always complaining to others about how overworked and underpaid they are. They frequently blame their failure on other people or the organisational systems, and may be sullen, irritable, impatient, argumentative, cynical and skeptical about everything. Authority figures often become the focus of discontent as the passive-aggressive person sees the authority figure as a significant cause of their problems. They may also resent people around them who do succeed. The passive-aggressive person may waver between open defiance and hostility toward an authority figure versus passive attempts to placate their supervisor by apologising and promising to improve their work performance. The passive-aggressive personality also likes to play win-lose games with others, and is always aiming to win as this makes them feel good about themselves and their ability.

Jane was an editor for a publishing house. She was always complaining about how overworked she was, constantly reminded her colleagues that she had too much work to review and too little time. When she was given a manuscript to work on, she would promise to deliver it by a certain time, and then fail to return the work by the promised date. She would tell management that the work required only small modifications and then at the last minute the manuscript would be returned with major changes that would take the author a considerable period of time to rework. In an industry working to very strict deadlines this was not appreciated, and people became frustrated with her. Her colleagues resented her behaviour as they ended up having to do a lot of the work she was responsible for. Jane vacillated between being extremely apologetic and pleading for people to be understanding versus open hostility towards colleagues for giving her so much work to do in the first place.

Narcissistic personality disorder

Sigmund Freud used the term narcissistic to describe people who showed an exaggerated sense of self-importance and a pre-occupation with receiving attention. The essential feature of narcissistic personality disorder is a pervasive pattern of grandiosity, the constant need for admiration and a lack of empathy for others.

Narcissistic people commonly overestimate their abilities and embellish their achievements, often coming across as boastful and conceited. They can become agitated or angry when people do not show them the respect and 'reverence' they believe they deserve. The narcissistic person fantasises about unlimited success, power, brilliance, beauty or idealised love. They also see themselves on par with famous people in terms of their achievements, and therefore expect to be treated the same as other 'stars'.

The narcissist believes that they are superior to other people and they boost their self-esteem by associating with people who are successful. For example, the narcissistic person will insist on having only the best doctor, lawyer, personal fitness instructor, hairdresser, membership of the best clubs, gyms, and so on.

The person with narcissistic personality disorder has a very fragile self-esteem because it revolves around constantly receiving admiration from other people. They like to show off their possessions to make others envious, and often openly seek compliments from people they are with. It is not unusual for them to unreasonably expect favourable treatment, such as being given the best table in a restaurant, parking wherever they want, or not having to line up to enter a nightclub. This sense of entitlement, combined with a lack of sensitivity to the wants and needs of others may lead to behaviour that exploits other people. However, this exploitation is not deliberately callous, it is simply a by-product of their need for admiration and special treatment. This fragile self-esteem makes the narcissistic person vulnerable to criticism from other people. Though they do not always show their feelings, criticism may leave them feeling empty, humiliated and degraded. They may react to criticism or perceived criticism with rage, counter-attack or disdain.

The narcissistic person does not have a great deal of success when it comes to recognising the desires and feelings of other people as they are too pre-occupied with themselves and their own feelings. They often do not consider other people's needs, and frequently make insensitive remarks about a variety of things. For example, they may talk about how great their own health is to a person who is chronically ill in hospital.

The narcissist is often jealous of other people. They do not like it when people appear to be more success-ful than they are, believing that they should be the recipient of such success. They frequently minimise the contributions of other people who receive awards, and are described by others as arrogant and conde-scending.

Narcissistic personality disorder is estimated to occur in less than 1 per cent of the population. Of people with the disorder, about 50 to 75 per cent are males. They differ from the psychopath because their behaviour is driven by a need for admiration from other people as opposed to enjoyment of other people's suffering. Regardless of the different motiva-tion, both the narcissist and the psychopath have the capacity to cause significant psychological damage to co-workers.

Jeremy was a lawyer in his early forties. He worked for a large law firm, and had all the trappings of success that went with his job – an expensive car, a house in an affluent part of the city and a series of attractive girl-friends (who did not go out with him for long at all). Jeremy described himself as a key player in the law firm (despite the fact he had been overlooked for partnership). He also exaggerated his achievements as a sportsman, indicating that when he finished school it was a difficult choice about whether to become a professional sportsman or a highly successful commercial lawyer. There was no evidence to support these claims.

Jeremy talked endlessly to colleagues about his visions of himself as a partner, making millions of dollars for the company and saving his clients from multi-million dollar law suits through his consummate skill as a lawyer. The reality was that Jeremy was not trusted by the law firm partners to handle anything more than routine, uncomplicated cases involving relatively small sums of money. Jeremy could not understand why he had been passed over for partnership, as he believed he was special. He told other people that the law firm was waiting for a big enough case to come along that would really use his skills.

Jeremy was also the cause of legal secretaries resigning or demanding transfers. He constantly looked for praise, and when it didn't happen he would became angry, taking it out on the legal secretaries, deliberately giving them too much work. He also blamed the legal secretaries for his own failure to produce work. His co-workers saw him as arrogant and condescending. When he was told that he was to work with an organisational consultant to develop a management plan, he agreed as he thought he was being groomed for a senior position. He insisted that the consultant be a well-recognised expert – that he 'only went to the best because winners attract winners'.

Histrionic personality disorder

Histrionic personality disorder refers to a condition where an individual is over-dramatic about everything and almost appears to be acting rather than genuinely experiencing things. People with histrionic personality disorder tend to be vain, extravagant and seductive. They often express emotion in an exaggerated way, such as sobbing uncontrollably at a sad movie or hugging someone they have just met as though they are long-lost friends. They are uncomfortable when they are not the centre of attention. They can be over-concerned about their looks and spend large amounts of money on clothing and jewellery.

The person with histrionic personality disorder is also fairly impulsive and has difficulty delaying self-gratification. They may have shallow and rapidly shifting emotions, while interaction with other people is often characterised by inappropriate sexually seductive or provocative behaviour. This provocative behaviour is not limited to relationships or close partners, it can be seen at work and on social occasions. They frequently consider relationships more intimate than they actually are.

Sufferers may seek to control people through emotional manipulation on one level, yet simultaneously they depend on them for attention on another level. They also have trouble with friends of the same sex as they are often seen as trying to 'steal' friends' partners through their provocative behaviour.

It is estimated that 2 to 3 per cent of the population may have the disorder. Males and females are equally likely to have histrionic personality disorder according to some studies. However these proportions are based on limited data.

The difference between histrionic personality disorder and psychopathy is that psychopaths manipulate for profit, power or other material gratification whereas histrionics manipulate to gain nurturance from those around them.

Schizophrenia

Schizophrenia is a mental disorder in which an individual experiences a psychotic episode. Diagnosis requires at least two or more positive, negative, and/or disorganised symptoms be present for at least one month.

Positive symptoms include the more active manifestations of abnormal behaviour, such as delusions or hallucinations. A delusion is a belief that would be seen by most members of society to be a misrepresentation of reality. For example, a belief that one is famous or a belief that people are trying to sabotage one's efforts. A hallucination is where a person experiences a sensory event without input from the surrounding environment. For example, a person hears a voice that is not really there. Auditory hallucinations are most common, and the imagined voices often give instructions.

Negative symptoms show an absence or insufficiency of normal behaviour, such as emotional and social withdrawal, apathy and lack of thought or speech. People with this symptom show little interest in performing even the most basic day-to-day functions, including those associated with personal hygiene. There are a few different types of negative symptoms. Alogia refers to the relative absence of speech. A person with alogia may respond to questions with very brief replies that may have little content, and they may appear uninterested in the conversation. Anhedonia is a presumed lack of pleasure experienced by some people with schizophrenia. It includes indifference to activities that are typically considered pleasurable including eating, social interactions, and sexual relations. Affective flattening is where a person does not demonstrate emotion where they would be expected to. They may stare vacantly at you, speak in a flat and toneless manner, and seem unaffected by things going on around them. However, they may be responding on the inside despite a lack of external reaction.

Disorganised symptoms includes disorganised speech, inappropriate affect and disorganised behaviour. Disorganised speech includes tangentiality where a person loses track of a question and goes off in another direction. For example, if a person is asked 'Why are you in the hospital?' they may reply 'I really don't want to be here. I have other things to do. The time is right you know, and when opportunity knocks...' The question is not really answered. Loose association or derailments are also features of disorganised speech. Essentially this involves changing topic or idea in mid-sentence. It is unclear if this is because the person does not understand the question, cannot focus their attention, or finds it too difficult to talk about a topic. Disorganised behaviour and inappropriate affect can include laughing or crying at inappropriate times, hoarding objects, or acting in unusual ways in public. Other 'active' behaviours that may be unusual include catatonia (motor dysfunction ranging from wild agitation to immobility), pacing uncontrollably or moving one's fingers or arms in stereotyped ways.

> Max was a thirty-year-old male who was working in a store selling office supplies. He experienced auditory hallucinations and paranoid delusions. While he was working he became increasingly paranoid that certain customers were trying to deliberately harm him. On one occasion, he confronted a male customer and accused him of trying to harm him. The man protested his innocence, and Max heard voices telling him to kill the man. Max seriously assaulted the man and had to be pulled away by shocked co-workers.

There are a number of people in the community who hold a job and suffer from schizophrenia or some other type of psychotic disorder. Many people with schizophrenia take medication to manage the condition and function at work. There are a small minority who do not take their medication, or who do not recognise they are experiencing a psychotic episode and may be dangerous to themselves and/or other people they work with or for.

Pathological gambling

Pathological gambling is where a person is preoccupied with gambling to the extent that they are unable to control, cut back or stop the gambling behaviour. They are constantly thinking about how to get more money to gamble with. It is not unusual for pathological gamblers to justify stealing money or defrauding a company of funds to 'win back' the money they have lost in their last gambling bout behaviour. Most people who are addicted to gambling say it is the aroused or excited state associated with taking risks and winning that drives them, rather than the money.

Pathological gamblers often lie to family, friends, co-workers and employers to hide the extent of their involvement with gambling. The pathological gambler is also prone to cognitive distortions such as super-stition, denial and over-confidence. The false belief in their ability to influence the outcome of their gambling behaviour generally leads to larger amounts of debt as they lose more money over time.

The pathological gambler is often highly competi-tive, energetic, restless and easily bored. At work they may be workaholics who thrive on the pressure of completing work just before a deadline. They are also capable of setting up elaborate schemes to obtain money without being noticed for considerable periods of time. This means that when the pathological gambler is finally discovered, the organisation has usually lost a great deal of money. The urge to gamble usually increases during periods of stress or depression. Stress can be caused by significant gambling losses, which lead to a vicious cycle in which the gambler tries to recoup their losses, becomes increasingly stressed, and consequently loses more money.

Police officers who specialise in fraud investigation recognise that a significant proportion of white-collar fraud behaviour is driven by gambling addictions, and to a lesser extent drug addiction.

Steven was an accountant who enjoyed betting. He had been working with the same firm for many years, had a wife and two children, and felt he was trapped in the hum-drum of suburban life. Steven's only form of relief, in his mind, was the time he spent at the casino or down at the racetrack with friends while he had 'a few beers'.

Initially this gambling behaviour was not a serious problem. He held down his job, paid all the bills and lived life normally. After a few years of enjoying his gambling behaviour, he started betting alone with larger sums of money. He lost a lot of money and had to hide this from his wife. Steven decided that he could fraudulently write cheques to himself from the company to cover his gambling debts. He was not caught the first time, and told himself it would never happen again. However, he could not resist the lure of gambling, and wrote additional cheques to himself for large amounts until a company audit detected his behaviour. He was arrested and charged, lost his job and his wife divorced him, moving interstate with his children.

Don't jump to conclusions – over diagnosis and confirmatory bias

It is important to be aware of psychopathic behaviours and characteristics along with other extreme personality types to protect ourselves and to avoid conflict. However, it is equally important not to jump to conclusions or try to diagnose someone's behaviour without professional advice.

Misdiagnosis or improper use of a label is just as destructive for a person as a psychopath can be. There is a phenomenon known as confirmatory bias that is very important when it comes to people making judgments about whether a colleague is a workplace psychopath versus 'something else'.

Confirmatory bias is a term used in social psychology that refers to an error in how people make judgments about various situations. Generally speaking, confirmatory bias occurs where a person 'confirms' what they want to believe by selectively looking at certain bits of information available to them.

For example, a person may believe that they are working with a psychopath, therefore they read a book such as this one to find out more about the workplace psychopath. The person reads through all of the characteristics carefully, and then looks for those characteristics in their colleague. They try and remember behaviours that their colleague has done which fit the characteristics they have read about. They may remember that 'Bob had an affair twenty years ago with a secretary, therefore he is sexually promiscuous and fits that criteria', an incorrect conclusion. In effect they find what they want to find, and ignore any contradictory evidence. Confirmatory bias is very dangerous as it can lead to 'false positives'; concluding that a person is a workplace psychopath when in fact they are not.

It is important to remember in psychology (and science in general) that one must always try and disprove rather than prove a theory. There is a famous example used in science that illustrates why. If a scientist has a theory that 'all birds in the world are black', how does he or she go about validly testing that theory. There are two possibilities.

First, they can try and prove the theory by travelling the world and looking only for black birds, incorrectly concluding that their theory is true when they do not notice birds of any other colour because they are not looking for them.

Second, and more valid, is to travel the world and try to find a bird that is not black. In other words, the theory is tested by trying to disprove it rather than confirm it.

If a reader believes that they are working with a psychopath of any sub-type, they should go about trying to disprove rather than prove their 'theory'. If they cannot disprove their 'theory' that the person is a workplace psychopath because the person fits many of the characteristics after careful consideration of the evidence, then it is possible that the person they know may be a workplace psychopath. If the person does not fit sufficient characteristics, yet they are still 'dysfunctional' to work with, an alternate diagnosis may be more appropriate.

Regardless of the diagnosis, if the person is causing you to suffer in any way, it is important that you talk with people about the situation. This can be family, friends, or a professional. If you try and face the problem alone, and they are a workplace psychopath, you present a much easier target and will most likely suffer in the end.

EPILOGUE

THE IDEA OF PSYCHOPATHS operating in our work environment preys on the mind. There is no question that workplace psychopaths exist. The extent of the damage they cause is, however, largely unknown as very little research has been conducted in this area.

In my own consulting work I have seen the immense psychological devastation workplace psychopaths create for the people around them. It is no exaggeration to say that many victims I have spoken to leave a small part of their 'soul' behind as a result of the treatment meted out by the psychopath. Victims often lose their belief in themselves, their relationships, their hopes and dreams for a future they can no longer imagine, and in some cases their drive to enjoy life itself. When the workplace psychopath steals their victim's innocence, they steal everyone's innocence.

As a result of my own journey into the minds of

workplace psychopaths and their victims, two reasons for writing *Working with Monsters* emerged. The first was to provide victims with some factual information that may help them deal with their experiences. Victims are often not believed, or feel as though they are going 'crazy'. They are frequently made out to be a 'trouble-maker' or a 'serial complainer' who should just 'learn to deal with life'. However, by understanding how the mind of a workplace psychopath works, the reasons behind why they do what they do and the process of victim selection, I hope victims can see that there are people they can talk to and trust, and it is possible to emerge as a much stronger person.

The second reason was to unravel the factors that make up the workplace psychopath in order to educate others about their potential danger. Society cannot afford to ignore workplace psychopaths, and it is only through greater understanding that we can begin to tackle the problem. Until we address our silent acceptance of the workplace psychopath, I believe we are to some extent complicit in their behaviours through our own inaction. After all, what difference, if any, exists between the person who tacitly condones the workplace psychopath's behaviour and the workplace psychopath themselves?

Now that the workplace psychopath has been openly identified, I hope that *Working with Monsters* helps prevent them from ever being able to vicitmise another person again.

ACKNOWLEDGEMENTS

Writing a book such as *Working with Monsters* could only be accomplished with the help of many people, to whom I am deeply grateful. First and foremost I am indebted to the victims of workplace psychopaths who trusted me enough to share their experiences. They provided me with inspiration and an immense belief in the resilience of the human spirit to overcome all obstacles in the face of adversity. Similarly, the organisations that invited me to assess 'problem employees' must be thanked for the faith they placed in me to preserve the confidentiality of our meetings and for allowing me to share their successful strategies for the benefit of employees and organisations experiencing similar problems.

I would also like to thank the many students from the University of Sydney who have attended my lectures over the years. I appreciate you sharing your experiences and thank you for raising many questions that I may not have otherwise explored.

Equally, I would like to thank my colleagues in the New South Wales Police force for showing me what it means to be a good investigator. To the two officers who opened up the world of fraud investigations, I am deeply grateful, this book would not have been nearly as effective without your assistance. To the detectives with whom I have worked on investigations, I am deeply indebted to you for showing me a world that I would otherwise not have known about when it comes to the mechanics of investigating serious violent crime. For security and/or operational reasons these officers cannot be named, but you know who you are. Thank you!

Thanks also to the team at Random House. In particular, to Jeanne Ryckmans for being so patient and believing in the idea of a book about psychopaths in the workplace; to Jody Lee for her very helpful editing; and to Lydia Papandrea for her tireless work with so many aspects of the book. It simply would not have been possible without your amazing support.

Last, but certainly not least, I would like to thank my family and friends for being there for me over the years. Again, this book would not have been possible without your support, encouragement and love. I could not ask for more loving family and friends and I am privileged to have all of you in my life.

BIBLIOGRAPHY

Babiak, Paul (1995). 'When psychopaths go to work: A case study of an industrial psychopath', *Applied Psychology: An International Review*, Vol. 44, 171–188.

Blackburn, R. (2000). *The Psychology of Criminal Conduct: Theory, Research and Practice*. Chichester: John Wiley & Sons.

Blair, R. (2001). 'Neurocognitive models of aggression, the antisocial personality disorders, and psychopathy', *Journal of Neurology, Neurosurgery and Psychiatry*, Vol. 76, 727–731.

Britton, P. (1997). *The Jigsaw Man*. London: Bantam Press.

Clarke, J.P. 'Challenging the Assumptions Underlying Offender Profiling of Australian Sexual Homicide Offenders: Offender Development, Crime Scene Behaviour, and Profiler Experiential Knowledge', Unpublished PhD Thesis; University of Sydney.

Clarke, John and Shea, Andy (2001). *Touched by the Devil*. Sydney: Simon & Schuster.

Cleckley, Dr Hervey M. (1976). *The Mask of Sanity*. St Louis: Mosby, 5th ed. (original work published in 1941).

Damasio, Antonio (2000). 'A neural basis for sociopathy', *Archives of General Psychiatry*, Vol. 57, 127–128.

Douglas, J.E., Ressler, R.K., Burgess, A.W. and Hartman, C.R. (1986). 'Criminal profiling from crime scene analysis', *Behavioral Sciences and the Law*, Vol. 4, 401–421.

Hamer, M. (2001). 'Personality characteristics and superior sales performance', *Dissertation Abstracts International: Sciences and Engineering*, Vol 62(5B).

Hare, Dr Robert D. (1991). *The Hare Psychopathy Checklist–Revised*. Toronto: Multi-Health Systems.

Hare, Dr Robert D. (1993). *Without Conscience: The Disturbing World of the Psychopaths Among Us*. New York: Pocket Books.

Hazelwood, Roy and Michaud, Steven (2001). *Dark Dreams: Sexual Violence, Homicide and the Criminal Mind*. New York: St Martins Press.

Keppel, R.D. and Birnes W.J. (1999). *Signature Killers*. New York: Pocket Books.

Krafft-Ebing, Richard von (1965). *Psychopathia Sexualis: A Medico-Ferensic Study*. New York: G.P. Putnam's Sons (first unexpurgated edition in English; original work published in 1886).

Petraitis, Vikki and O'Connor, Chris (1999). *Rockspider*. Melbourne: Hybrid Publishers.

Raine, A., Lencz, T., Bihrle, S., LaCasse, L. and Colletti, P. (2000). 'Reduced prefrontal gray matter volume and reduced autonomic activity in anti-social personality disorder', *Archives of General Psychiatry*, Vol. 57, 119–127.

Ressler, R. and Schachtman, T. (1992). *Whoever Fights Monsters*. New York: St. Martin's Press.

Richards, Helene and Freeman, Sheila (2002). *Bullying in the Workplace: An Occupational Hazard*. Pymble, NSW: HarperCollins.

Serin, R.C. (1991). 'Psychopathy and violence in criminals', *Journal of Interpersonal Violence*, Vol. 4, 435–448.